THE BEHAVIOUR TOOLBAG

SUPPORTING CHANGE IN SCHOOLS

THE BEHAVIOUR TOOLBAG

Practical Strategies & Interventions

HINTON HOUSE PRACTICAL RESOURCES

John Murray
& Sonia Murray

HINTONHOUSE

Dedication

To Our Amazing Sons

We would like to dedicate this book to our two wonderful sons, Ryan and Calum. You have been our inspiration, our most important influence and our greatest teachers.

Published in 2024 by Hinton House Publishers, Park Farm, Preston Deanery, Northants NN7 2DY, United Kingdom

Tel: 01604 870828 Int Tel: +44 (0) 1604 870828

www.hintonpublishers.com

British Library Cataloguing in Publication Data

A catalogue record for this book is available from the British Library

ISBN: 978 1906531 270

CONTENTS

ACKNOWLEDGEMENTS

In the journey of writing this book, we have been fortunate to be surrounded by a circle of incredible individuals whose support and encouragement have been pivotal.

First and foremost, our deepest gratitude goes to our amazing families and, in particular, our boys, Ryan and Calum. Their unwavering faith in us, endless patience, and boundless love have been the cornerstone of our strength and motivation that has enabled us to achieve our vision. They have celebrated our triumphs and offered comfort during challenges, always reminding us of the importance of pursuing our passions.

To the children and families we have had the honour of working with over the years: your stories, resilience and joy have been a constant source of inspiration. You have taught us invaluable lessons and have been the real-life heroes of our journey. Your impact extends far beyond the pages of this book, touching our hearts in ways words can scarcely capture.

A heartfelt acknowledgement is due to the myriad of professionals we have had the privilege of collaborating with. Their dedication, expertise and innovative thinking have been a wellspring of inspiration. These individuals, from diverse fields and backgrounds, have enriched our perspectives and greatly contributed to our growth both personally and professionally. Their commitment to excellence and their spirit of collaboration have been nothing short of inspirational.

We reserve special thanks to Brian Kettleborough (Headteacher) and Hilary Gooding (Behaviour Support Consultant), whose belief and trust in us have been monumental. Brian, your knowledgeable insights and strategic thinking have guided us through our journey with clarity and purpose. Hilary, your depth of knowledge and unwavering love and support have continually fuelled our passion. Both of you saw something in us, encouraged us relentlessly and inspired us to persevere in our work with children and their families. Your confidence in our abilities and your constant encouragement have been key in our pursuit of this endeavour. We are forever grateful for your invaluable contributions and the faith you have placed in us.

To all of you, your presence in our lives is a gift we cherish deeply. This book is not just a reflection of our efforts but a testament to the love, support and guidance you have generously offered us. Thank you from the bottom of our hearts.

ABOUT THE AUTHORS

John Murray is a highly qualified and experienced professional in the field of education, with a background that includes roles as a Teacher, Manager of a Behaviour Support Service and former Ofsted Inspector. With over 35 years working in and collaborating with schools and various agencies, including a special school for children experiencing social, emotional and mental health difficulties (SEMH), John has established himself as an expert in his field. His qualifications include a BA (Hons) B. Phil in Education and NPQH.

John's career has been centred around working with children and young people facing a spectrum of challenges, including social, emotional, mental health, relational, and behavioural issues. He has held several senior management positions in schools and other settings, including a local authority. In all of these positions, John has been instrumental in providing strategic direction and developing policy in regard to behaviour support services.

Renowned as an experienced trainer, John has an excellent reputation for designing and delivering courses that provide theoretical insights and are deeply rooted in the practical application of behaviour support techniques.

John's expertise extends to being an experienced Team Teach trainer for nearly two decades and he is currently a Principal Team Teach Trainer. As a founder and director of Jogo Behaviour Support, John is keen on fostering partnerships to develop and provide services that meet the diverse needs associated with behavioural issues.

Sonia Murray is a distinguished Behaviour Support Consultant and Play Therapist, exemplifying over three decades of dedicated service in various critical aspects of child development and mental health. Her qualifications, including a Diploma in Social Work (DipSW) and registration as a Play Therapist, underscore her commitment to professional excellence.

Sonia's expertise spans a remarkable range of areas, notably in attachment, child abuse, social, emotional and behavioural difficulties, children's mental health, childhood trauma, parenting programmes and Play Therapy. She is a practitioner and a highly sought-after trainer, sharing her invaluable insights nationally and internationally on subjects such as attachment, trauma, play therapy, understanding behaviour, play, communication with children, behaviour management and positive parenting.

With a career spanning over 35 years, Sonia has been a childcare social worker, parent worker and Play Therapist in various settings such as education, social care and health. Notably, she has dedicated 22 years to a specialist school for children with complex social, emotional, mental health and behavioural difficulties.

In addition to her hands-on roles, Sonia provides consultation, supervision and training in both statutory and voluntary sectors of children's services. She is a visiting lecturer at the University of Roehampton.

Sonia is also an accomplished author, contributing significantly to the field with publications and chapters in notable works.

She is a founder and director of Jogo Behaviour Support. For more information please visit **www.jogobehavioursupport.com**

INTRODUCTION

You cannot change a plug with a hammer. But that does not mean the hammer is intrinsically a bad tool. We need to have as large a toolbag with as many tools as we can. Sometimes, to develop the most appropriate responses to behaviour, it is the process of choosing the right tool from the toolbag.

This book is a culmination of our combined 75 years of lived professional experiences, skills developed over that time and accumulated knowledge. Our worlds connected over 30 years ago when we met in a school where pupils displayed and communicated distress through their behaviours. It was a challenge to develop and implement appropriate responses. The resources available to us were limited. The building was an old Georgian house, not a purposely designed school for pupils experiencing social, emotional, mental health and behavioural difficulties, and made teaching and learning difficult. However, over time, with a little creativity and a lot of hard work, we created a holistic learning environment. The uniqueness of the learning environment we made and the methodology we brought to our delivery was that one of us approached the situation from a teacher's perspective and the other approached it from a psychological viewpoint. It has proved a useful combination that endeavours to see, feel, hear and support the pupils who have entered our world. While having slightly different perspectives, we share the same view that the pupil's needs should be at the centre of everything we do. We have the same passion, belief and ethos for understanding the individual pupil and finding the best approach to meet their needs. The pupils we taught have been our greatest teachers and some of the most incredible practitioners we have been fortunate enough to work with. Each and every one of them has influenced our practices.

Our paths differ slightly, but the combination provides a holistic approach to supporting behaviour. The accumulation of these approaches and the wonderful teachers who have influenced us have enabled us to create Jogo Behaviour Support. Jogo Behaviour Support is a specialist company providing a holistic approach to supporting children experiencing social, emotional, mental health and behavioural challenges. Our experience and knowledge have led us to realise that to foster change, we need to support all the systems around the child. This includes working directly with the child and supporting their family, their teachers, the school and others in the child's life. While school can facilitate great change it is only one aspect of children's lives. Consequently, we understand the necessity of engaging with as many aspects of the child's life as possible to facilitate sustained change.

By offering a range of services from Jogo Behaviour Support's experienced multidisciplinary team of teachers, social workers and therapists, we can utilise their eclectic knowledge and skills to create bespoke approaches for each individual situation. We offer behaviour support to schools and families and provide therapeutic support, including play therapy and family support. Additionally, Jogo Behaviour Support delivers a range of training courses to enhance practitioners' practice.

Why this book

We wanted to write this book because of the pupils we worked with. It is not merely an attempt to discuss ways of supporting behaviour but to go beyond the behaviour, to see the child, and affect change so they can succeed, learn and grow. Managing behaviour without understanding what influences it will get us only so far. This book considers the topic of behaviour in as wide a context as possible. It begins with looking at why it is important to clearly define behaviours and develop a culture where behaviour can flourish to support teaching and learning. It looks at the influences on behaviour, different types of behaviour and the importance of relationships between adults and pupils. There are also practical elements to explore in the book, such as how we develop responses to behaviour.

At the book's core is the exploration of how, as practitioners, we can affect and influence behaviour and even change it when necessary. This is done by looking at a range of strategies and interventions and measuring effectiveness through a target-setting process. However, strategies and interventions can only be successful when the environment for them to flourish is established. Hopefully, this book will provide you with additional skills and knowledge or tools for your professional toolbag. While this is an important aspect of the book, the process of choosing a particular tool at any one time will be looked at, alongside when and how we should implement it. This is because choosing the correct tool can be just as important as its application; it depends on many factors, not least trying to understand the driving need before we support the behaviour. Choose the wrong tool and the implementation will not succeed. You cannot change a plug with a saw.

The strategies and interventions, styles of approach and the process of how and why we develop responses to behaviour discussed in this book are, in essence, an attempt to chart a path that adheres to directly meeting the child's needs. Some may advocate an approach broadly seen as behaviourist, primarily relying on tools related to boundaries, structured routine, rules, rewards and consequences. Others prefer an approach more aligned with theories and research on nurture, attachment, social and emotional issues, and trauma-informed responses. We believe that one approach should not exclude the other and there is a place for both – a middle way where both approaches work together in the learning environment to meet the needs of all pupils.

CHAPTER 1

The Teacher: One of the Greatest Influences on Behaviour

> *'Those who know do, those who understand teach.'*
> Aristotle

> An understanding heart is everything in a teacher and cannot be esteemed highly enough. One looks back with appreciation to the brilliant teachers, but with gratitude to those who touched our human feeling. The curriculum is so much necessary raw material, but warmth is the vital element for the growing plant and for the soul of the child. (Jung, 1954, p. 144)

Bambaeeroo and Shokrpour (2017) investigated the impact of teachers' non-verbal communication on success in teaching and discovered that pupil/teacher relationships were pivotal. The findings of this study also indicate that non-verbal communication skills can play an important role in the future of a pupil's life. All of us can remember our favourite teacher and our worst teacher. Either can have a lasting influence on us. Teachers are the cornerstone for behaviour management. They are the most important strategy and intervention. You can have the cleverest strategies and interventions, but if they are not delivered with confidence, clarity, consistency, persistency and compassion, they will not be effective. The teacher's presence sets the agenda for the learning environment. Section 7 of the Department for Education's (DfE's) Teachers' Standards (2011) – 'Manage behaviour effectively to ensure a good and safe learning environment' – states that a teacher must:

- have clear rules and routines for behaviour in classrooms, and take responsibility for promoting good and courteous behaviour both in classrooms and around the school, in accordance with the school's behaviour policy

- have high expectations of behaviour, and establish a framework for discipline with a range of strategies, using praise, sanctions, and rewards consistently and fairly
- manage classes effectively, using approaches which are appropriate to pupils' needs in order to involve and motivate them
- maintain good relationships with pupils, exercise appropriate authority, and act decisively when necessary.

The last point on exercising authority is possibly the one that is open to most interpretation. How much authority is appropriate when 'exercising appropriate authority'? One interpretation could lead to a perception of a slightly dictatorial view of classroom management, where the teacher's job is to control behaviour and quell insurrection. However, if viewed through the approach of Lee Canter's *Assertive Discipline* (Canter & Canter, 1992), we are able to put the concept of exercising authority into a more useful context. The key aspect of this model is that teachers have a right to teach and must be allowed to engage the pupils in the learning environment, in the same way that pupils have a right to learn. This is achieved by setting clear rules, supported by rewards and consequences. To deliver this approach, Canter & Canter believed that teachers in a classroom should explain consistently and continually; they should also practice and model expectations and procedures to create an effective learning environment.

In contrast, Susannah Temple's (2005) model of 'functional fluency' suggests an alternative way of understanding what 'exercising appropriate authority' looks like. Temple (2005, p.11) states:

> 'The model puts emphasis on positive ways of being in charge and using authority, helping teachers to learn more ways to empower and care for their pupils so that they become more self-confident and more self-disciplined. It is vital to get away from the argument over whether it is better to be 'harder' or 'softer' on pupils and realise that the key issue is how to exert authority that is both strict and kind, and always respectful.'

In Temple's view, a teacher cannot 'control' behaviour. However, they can create an environment and relationships that invite cooperation and positive, spontaneous self-expression. A good teaching and learning environment cannot occur if the teachers are:

- dominant: negative, critical and using fear of their power to motivate pupils

or

- marshmallowing: over-scaffolding, over-present and not allowing pupils to exercise the level of independence appropriate to their stage of emotional and intellectual development.

Either of these will only create a room full of passive, compliant pupils at best or, at worst, lead to disruptive behaviours.

What both approaches have in common is that the teacher needs to portray confidence and authority with their presence. Canter & Canter (1992) may be more explicit in defining clear boundaries, while Temple (2005) is more specific on avoiding displays of dominance that may lead to confrontation. Canter & Canter (1992) would call this style 'assertive', while Temple would express that the teacher should possess a strong sense of self-assurance regarding their identity and their capacity to establish positive connections with others.

The teacher's presence and style will be central to the appropriate way of exercising authority. This is not an attempt to stifle the individuality or personality of a teacher, but recognises that how we deliver our teaching in the learning environment will affect how the pupils access their learning. It is hoped that teachers will aspire to being assertive, confident and assured, while approaching events calmly and with consistency. However, there may be occasions, particularly when dealing with incredibly challenging situations, when our style of approach suffers. When this happens, a change in the teacher's style can make strategies and interventions less effective.

It is useful to consider the different styles. Canter & Canter identified three styles of approach (Canter &

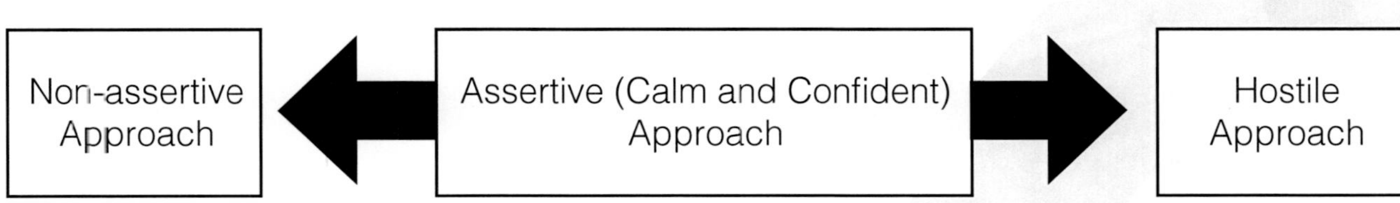

Canter 1992): Assertive (Calm and Confident), Non-assertive and Hostile. It helps to think about them on a continuum.

The Non-assertive Approach

This style is based on the perception that exercising control can be done best if the teacher is liked, popular and almost seen as a friend. It is open to misinterpretation by the pupil, as they will view their position as equal to the teacher's, making it difficult for the teacher to exercise authority. There is also the possibility the pupil will perceive the teacher as weak and unable to exercise authority. When that authority has to be introduced, it communicates lack of confidence; this may be demonstrated in body language that is powerless and portrays a sense of giving up. The tone of voice can sound like a plea or request, rather than a clear instruction. The basic behaviour plan in the learning environment lacks clarity; rules are not established, rewards unclear and consequences uncertain. This approach makes the pupil feel unsure of the teacher's response in any given situation as the style is inconsistent. As the boundaries of the learning environment are unclear, some pupils may feel, at best, hypervigilant, insecure and unsure or, at worst, emotionally unsafe. The outcomes of this approach will make it difficult to manage behaviour, establish authority and implement the behaviour plan.

Real-life example

Child behaviour: pupil tapping their pencil and rocking back and forth on their chair

Non-assertive teacher responses:

- "Do you think it is a good idea to do that?"
- "Can you stop?"
- "I would be pleased if you stopped."
- "Why are you …?"

The script is unclear and confusing. The tone of voice comes across as unconfident and pleading. The body language communicates lack of confidence, fear and frustration.

The relationship is based on the pupil controlling the events.

The Hostile Approach

This style of approach is based on the perception that to exercise authority you must win, stand up to pupils and not lose face in any circumstance. The hostile approach demands respect rather than earning it. The structures that contribute to the atmosphere of the learning environment are imposed and pupils have little ownership. Communication from the teacher to pupils can be confrontational and sarcastic or even degrading and, in the worst-case scenario, threatening or abusive. Body language is negative and the approach is reactive – we could argue 'lazy', as there is no attempt at building the relationship. This approach acts on feelings about or perceptions of a pupil and is based on who is liked or disliked. The outcomes are a learning environment where trust between the teacher and the pupil is lacking, the atmosphere is not conducive to learning, engagement levels are low, conflict levels are high and pupils feel uncomfortable.

Real-life example

Child behaviour: pupil tapping their pencil and rocking back and forth on their chair

Hostile teacher responses:

- "I do not intend to ask you again."
- "If you do not stop, I will make sure you do not have a playtime for the rest of the week."
- "Your behaviour is not fair to the others who want to learn."
- "Right, that is it, I have had enough of you!"

The script is based on anger and emotion. The body language can be seen as aggressive and the tone is angry.

The Assertive (Confident and Calm) Approach

This is a style based on mutual respect and a clear understanding of what is expected of the teacher and the pupil in the learning environment. The approach is one that is calm, controlled, consistent and clear. The exercise of authority is a planned approach. It is not reactive to events or situations. The teacher has high expectations of pupils. The boundaries are clear, as is the behaviour plan. This approach actively teaches the rules, uses rewards appropriately and consequences fairly. It is an approach that creates a sense of safety for the learner, who can be challenged in a supportive atmosphere. The teacher spends time building relationships and understanding the individual needs of the pupil. The outcome is a teacher who feels in control and knows why, when and how to exercise authority. The importance of style and approach cannot be underestimated as it will set the atmosphere in the learning environment, determine how the relationship between teacher and pupil develops, and enhance the implementation of the behaviour plan.

Real-life example

Child behaviour: pupil tapping their pencil and rocking back and forth on their chair

Assertive teacher responses:

- "You need to keep four legs of the chair on the ground."
- "You need to put the pen on the desk." (Gives the pupil a clear direction on how they should be using the pen.)
- Uses proximity praise to those who are sitting still or using the pen appropriately.

The script is clear. The tone of voice and the body language communicate confidence and the expectation that the actions will be undertaken.

Creating a confident and calm approach is reliant on the teacher's presence and their reflective ability to understand themselves, their bodies, their feelings and their thoughts. All of which can be learnt.

The Teacher's Presence

'Teachers depend on a receptive audience to trigger their own positive biochemistry and brain growth.'

(Cozolino, 2013, p. 50)

Presence is defined as 'a quality that makes people notice or admire you, even when you are not speaking' (Cambridge University Press, 2022a). Many other professions utilise presence to gain the best performance, whether this involves acting, selling a product or trying to convey a political view. This is a skill that some argue should be integrated into teacher training (Salter, 2016). Cuddy (2012) defines having presence as being authentic, captivating, enthusiastic, passionate, confident and comfortable. By using a confident presence, we convey sincerity. All of us can name teachers whose confident presence has impacted on us. They are the ones who have inspired me to achieve my best and/or to love a subject that we knew little about. I (Sonia) had to study social policy during my social work training, which was a subject that had little interest for me. However, the teacher and his presence bought the subject alive and helped me to understand the value of my role in collaborating with people.

The teacher's presence refers to how they present themselves to their pupils in their role of teacher (they may present differently in their other roles, such as of parent or friend). It involves the teacher's body language and their voice, including their tone and their words. This comes from their internal perception of themselves, individually and as a teacher. A major component of communication and the portrayal of safety is body language. As humans, our instincts require us to assess for danger – the body language and facial expressions of those around us are the biggest indicators of threat. However, to turn that on its head, body language and facial expressions are also the largest pointers of safety. If used effectively, they can portray to pupils that their teacher is a safe adult and the learning environment is a safe place. Our body language and facial expressions will convey when we are feeling anxious, frightened or angry – unless we consciously choose to override this and communicate confidence. Children are genetically wired to be reliant on their carers to provide physical and emotional safety. As noted by Cozolino (2013, p.18), 'the position of the teacher is very similar to that of the parent in building a child's brain. Both can enhance a child's emotional regulation by providing a safe haven that supports the learning process'. As teachers are in loco parentis or in other words are responsible for the pupils while their parents are absent, they must behave as any reasonable parent would to enhance the wellbeing and safety of pupils in their care (Children Act, 1989).

As children, we were both taught that the key to becoming more confident was to portray self-belief, even if we were not feeling it: to hold our heads up high, stand up straight, make eye contact, have a firm handshake and, most importantly, to smile right up to our eyes. We were both encouraged to do this even if we were going into a new and scary environment. This strategy did make things feel easier and we both developed in confidence. As Cuddy *et al* (2012) state, 'our mind changes our bodies, but our bodies can change our minds'. By changing our body language we influence how we feel and think; conveying a confident presence, even if we are anxious inside, actually helps us to feel more confident within. Cuddy *et al* explored the impact of undertaking a high-power pose (standing tall with hands on hips) for two minutes prior to taking an evaluation. They found that the pupils who took the high-power pose performed better than pupils who adopted a low-power pose. Cuddy believes that you can 'fake it until you make it', but not only that – you can 'fake it until you become it. Do it enough until you actually become it and internalize it' (Cuddy *et al*, 2012).

There are a number of ways you can enhance your physical presence.

- Use a Duchenne smile – this is a smile that lifts the corners of the mouth, while engaging the orbicularis oculi muscles, which makes the cheeks rise and the corners of the eyes scrunch up. In other words, you smile right up to your eyes. This smile portrays enjoyment and trustworthiness.
- Stand in a grounded way, with feet hip-width apart.
- Stand with your back straight, head held high and shoulders hanging loosely.

- Keep your arms down by your sides and swinging naturally.
- Hold your hands open, with thumbs turned outwards.
- Notice how you are breathing and ensure that you are breathing slowly and into your diaphragm.
- Make eye contact.

Rodenburg's Exercise

Rodenburg's (2009) exercise about understanding your physical presence can be useful for teachers to see how they are perceived by their pupils and what non-verbal messages they may be portraying.

Get recent photos and videos of yourself. Examine your body, your head and shoulder position, your chest and abdomen and your legs, knees and feet in the images. Then consider the following:

- What do they portray to you?
- What do they portray to others?

Once you understand your presence, you can then look at tweaking it. Please refer to Rodenburg (2009) for further examples of developing your presence.

Not only is it important to understand your physical presence, but it is also necessary to understand the use of your tone of voice. Again, your tone of voice will portray your emotions and level of confidence, thus determining the sense of safety. When we are lacking in confidence, we may speak too fast, in a higher tone and sound out of breath as we may be shallow breathing. Additionally, we may raise our volume to a shouting point as we are becoming increasingly anxious or feel out of control. Every person who has been in a classroom has raised their volume to get the attention of the pupils, but how we present that raised volume can portray different things. If we do it from a reactive fear response, it can sound very different to when we purposely raise our volume from a confident stance. Even if the volume is the same, the impression will be very different and will depict separate messages.

Real-life example

We supported a teacher who was finding the behaviour of their class particularly challenging and had been advised not to shout as they had been perceived as shouting too much. They had then felt completely deskilled as they did not know how else to contain the class. Dwivedi (1997) notes that 'sometimes giving up certain behaviours (such as punitive ones) may feel like losing whatever power or control one has over the situation and can be associated with feelings of complete helplessness' (p.92). When we unpicked the shouting, the teacher was able to reflect that they often used shouting as a response to their rising fear of not being able to manage the class. Therefore, the shouting was a reactive response and would often depict their underlying fear. This was what was being picked up by others. We developed their assertive tone of voice that then illustrated their growing confidence.

Practice Point

Practising in front of a mirror, using a voice-recording app, can help develop the confident body stances and tones/volumes of voice.

Using our presence to deal with situations involving challenging behaviours

While it is essential to have a strong, confident teaching presence for your general teaching, it is also necessary to have it when you are dealing with situations regarding challenging behaviours. The prerequisite before implementing any behaviour strategy or intervention is to be aware of our presence. This includes understanding our own thoughts, feelings and bodily responses. Being aware of what different behaviours and managing behaviours trigger in us, enables us to respond from a thinking and calm state rather than a reactive state.

Our bodies, like those of the pupils, are designed to detect threat and keep us safe. They will respond to any perceived or actual threat quicker than our thinking brain. Therefore, being aware of our body's responses will provide us with information about our emotional state and the situation. A starting point is being conscious of our breath – where we are breathing in our body is important. If we are shallow breathing in our upper chest and our heart is beating faster than normal, it may indicate that our emotional state has changed. If our emotional state changes, it is more or less guaranteed that the pupil's state has changed or will change.

Our bodies and brains are often interconnected with others, particularly at stressful times. Therefore, if the teacher can regulate their emotional and bodily responses, then the pupil may begin to match them. By the teacher slowing their breath, which will calm them, thus enabling them to fully access their prefrontal cortex (thinking brain), they are able to respond from a regulated thinking state. Alongside this, the child's mirror neurons may begin to react to the regulated teacher and they then become more settled. Their breath may deepen and their heart rate can slow. Mirror neurons are neurons in the brain that respond when someone else is observed doing an action (Acharya & Shukla, 2012). This can sometimes lead the person to imitate the action and can be useful when dealing with challenging situations.

Real-life example

I (Sonia) was working individually with a pupil who the previous day had shown his dysregulation and distress by throwing paint everywhere, turning over a table and hurling a chair across the room. The next morning, I was conscious that I was feeling unsure, uncertain and nervous about how the session would go. Therefore, I undertook some breathing exercises to regulate and calm myself. I thought I had managed to settle. I walked the 20 metres to the pupil's classroom, collected him and we walked back to the small group intervention room. Once in the room, he turned to me and said, 'Why are you out of breath?' This shocked me, as he was absolutely right – I was shallow breathing and out of breath (not from the walk, but from my anxiousness about the upcoming session). He had picked it up from my body before I had become aware of it. I noticed that he was also shallow breathing. Had his mirror neurons picked this up off me or had my mirror neurons picked it up off him? Or it may have been a combination of how we were both feeling.

Reflection Point

Think of a time when you were having to support in a situation involving challenging behaviour. Note down your responses:

- Bodily responses: increased heart rate, sweating, shallow breathing, scanning the environment, stomach churning.
- Feeling responses: fear, dread, anger, frustration, disappointment, annoyance, sense of being deskilled, confusion.
- Thought responses: "Oh no, here we go again", "I don't know what to do", "Other people manage better than me", "I am fed up with this", "Whatever I do, it doesn't work".

Having considered these responses, think about and practise different options for the three areas:

- Bodily responses: slow your breath, breathe into your diaphragm, unclench fingers, use a strong body stance, lower your shoulders, etc.
- Feeling responses: notice the feelings – we may be unable to change them, but we can choose to respond to them from a regulated state.
- Thought responses: "I can do this", "This child is hurting somewhere", "They need me to be confident", "I can portray safety".

Understanding how we are reacting and feeling enables teachers to prepare for similar situations in the future.

The Learning Environment

We cannot look at the role of the teacher and the influence they have on behaviour without mentioning the environment where the interaction and relationship-building takes place. The classroom and how it is organised and utilised should not be discounted. The practicalities in a learning environment are important. Does the layout, the physical structure of the building, allow pupils to actively engage in the learning, behave appropriately, help them feel safe and secure? Is there sufficient space? Is the lighting adequate? Are the acoustics sufficient for all? Is there enough ventilation? Can the temperature be controlled? Is furniture arranged so movement is easily managed around the room? How accessible are resources? Are there enough resources? Is there wall space for displays that are interactive and reflective of pupil's work? Is the main teaching board easily viewed by all? Are materials labelled? Once these practical conditions are established, the attention can begin to focus on making sure the other conditions are in place.

Classroom checklist

- ❑ Staff are on time for pupils and in class before them.
- ❑ Support is available and accessible.
- ❑ Materials are prepared.
- ❑ Equipment is available and accessible.
- ❑ Routines are clearly established such as entering the classroom, movement around the room, getting the attention of the class/teacher, changing activities and/or transitions, going to the toilet, clearing up, leaving the room, what to do when an activity is finished, getting and putting away equipment.
- ❑ Furniture is arranged to best effect.
- ❑ A seating plan is in place.
- ❑ Materials are well labelled and located.
- ❑ The room is designed to allow pupils to move around.
- ❑ Storage of pupils' belongings is appropriate.
- ❑ Room organisation meets a variety of learners' needs.

- ❑ Staff communicate with a clear voice.
- ❑ Instructions and scripts are clear.
- ❑ Staff model appropriate behaviour.
- ❑ Staff acknowledge good behaviour.
- ❑ Staff recognise achievement among pupils.
- ❑ Staff name or define appropriate behaviour and reflect it back when pupils engage in it.
- ❑ The classroom behaviour plan is clear to all.
- ❑ Behaviour is seen as a responsibility of both the staff and pupils.
- ❑ Issues of concern are identified early and provision is made to meet needs.
- ❑ Rules are few in number and clearly displayed.
- ❑ Rules are understood by pupils, regularly referred to and reinforced.
- ❑ The behaviour required to meet rules is taught.
- ❑ Rewards are awarded fairly and consistently, are clearly related to positive behaviour, achievable and linked to the school system.
- ❑ Consequences are related to behaviour, are fair and consistently implemented.
- ❑ The hierarchy is gradual and graded and understood by pupils.

Final Thoughts

The teacher's presence, especially when dealing with situations involving challenging behaviours, is essential in creating a safe and productive learning environment for all in the classroom. We need to portray confidence and safety to enable pupils to feel safe enough to risk learning. Many challenging behaviours are driven by fear and if the teacher is frightened or anxious about dealing with them, this further exacerbates the pupil's fear, which can lead to an escalation. Often, we ask teachers to put on their 'cloak of confidence', even when they are feeling anxious. We have a natural presence, but it can be further enhanced, first by understanding ourselves, and then by practising some of the techniques in this chapter.

Learning Points

- Pupils need adults to be confident around them.
- The teacher's presence needs to portray safety and confidence.
- Our teacher presence can be learned.
- Our bodies can portray our internal state, but we can modulate our bodies to portray confidence.
- Only a regulated adult can calm a dysregulated child.

CHAPTER 2

The Importance of Relationships in Developing Behaviour Support Approaches and Responses

> *'They may forget what you said, but they will never forget how you made them feel.'*
> C.W. Buechner (1971)

Real-life example

When I first met Jimmy, he was raging round school and often assaulting school staff and other pupils. Any time anyone tried to get close to him either physically or relationally, he would erupt into challenging behaviours. He and everyone around him felt distressed and agitated. School staff were struggling to understand why their well-intentioned approaches were failing and were beginning to withdraw relationally from him. Everyone, including Jimmy, felt safer away from the relationship. However, this inadvertently reinforced his challenging behaviours because they were a protective strategy developed from his deep-seated fear of being in a relationship. Understanding this fear helped Jimmy's teachers to provide a careful relational behavioural plan to address the causes of his challenging behaviours.

One of the core foundation blocks of behaviour support is the development and sustaining of relationships within the learning environment. Humans are genetically made to form relationships. We are social animals and seek connections with others. It has always been accepted that the teacher-child relationship is a significant factor in the establishment of a successful learning environment. However, there have been tensions put on this relationship in recent times. This may be due to the constant pressure on both staff and pupils to succeed and meet the increasing demands of the achievement and attainment agenda.

The development of positive relationships, among all members of a school, is essential for building and maintaining a healthy learning environment. In the rush to identify a problem or concern and develop a plan to respond to the problem, it is often forgotten that managing or affecting the behaviour of another begins with establishing the relationship. It is important that we have constructive working relationships for all parties. If teaching staff do not feel connected with others, they are likely to be reluctant to want to come to work in the school. The same applies for all those involved, but most significantly for the pupils. Children and young people are reliant on adults' connections to help them feel safe and secure. The relationship between staff member and child is not only the starting point in developing all positive approaches to behaviour support, it is the golden thread that goes right through the process. The relationship affects how an issue or behaviour is perceived, how it is identified.

In a school or classroom, behaviour will occur/exist within the context of the relationships between all those with an interest in that learning environment. There will be varied and complex 'relationship units', and some will have a greater effect than others. There are many types of relationship unit. The term 'relationship unit' refers to the relationships between staff and the individual child, or between staff and groups of pupils, between different members of staff, or between different pupils, between staff and other professionals, between leadership teams and staff, or between staff and parents/carers. These relationship units not only affect the behaviour of those within that unit, but also the behaviour of others in a different unit.

Reflection Point

Take a moment to think about the relationship units that are in your working environment. Consider the role of these units and how they influence the learning environment.

The Teacher and Teaching Assistant Relationship Unit

The relationship between a teacher and the teaching assistant is a key relationship unit within a classroom. As individuals, the teacher and teaching assistant will establish their own relationship units but, together, the teacher/teaching assistant unit will establish a relationship unit with the class as a group. This unit will set the tone in the learning environment. It will be the means by which routines and the whole-class behaviour plan will be agreed. Behaviour will be modelled, expectations established, boundaries developed, clear methods of communication used and consistent practice implemented.

This relationship unit will operate as a team with clear objectives or outcomes, clear processes to support achievement of those outcomes, with a full understanding of what each party is doing during an activity in the learning environment. If this relationship unit is not well established or in fact non-existent, it will adversely affect the behaviour of the pupils in the learning environment. Communication will not be clear; the pupils will experience differing approaches, scripts and responses to similar behaviours, and differing expectations; boundaries will lack definition and a lack of consistency in approach will, at best, cause confusion. There may be some pupils who will take advantage of this confusion and try to take control. No amount of strategies or interventions will be able to flourish in such an environment.

> In *Teacher and Child: A Book for Parents and Teachers* (1972), Haim Ginnot states:
>
> 'I have come to the frightening conclusion I am the decisive element that creates the climate. It is my personal approach that creates the climate. It is my daily mood that makes the weather. As a teacher I possess tremendous power to make a child's life miserable or joyous. I can be a tool of torture or an instrument of inspiration. I can humiliate or humour, hurt or heal. In all situations, it is my response that decides whether a crisis will be escalated or deescalated and a child humanised.' (p.15)

Although some of the language in this extract may seem a little extreme, particularly the references to 'torture', 'hurt' and 'humiliate', the core idea is correct. The staff in the school, and particularly in the classroom, are the most significant dynamic and it is they who provide the foundations for productive learning and encourage productive activity within that learning environment. The staff set the agenda for what will happen, how it happens and when it happens. It is not about total control, as a productive environment needs all to feel a sense of ownership, but it is a recognition that the adults in the classroom are decisive in creating the conditions by which learning can take place.

Establishing working relationships

While it is essential to form relationship units in school, it is important that there are clear boundaries around the relationships. The core elements to these relationships are an understanding of the boundaries, clarity of role, empathy, understanding and care. The starting point of any relationship in schools is establishing a sense of safety and being clear about the parameters of the relationship. This is created in the term 'professional relationship'. The professional relationship is often based on the individuals' roles and determines how people behave with each other in those roles. Generally, the person delineates their role, their expectations, the boundaries of the relationship and conveys their willingness to connect. This is the same for a headteacher, class teacher, support staff, pupils and parents.

Real-life example: on a teacher's first day in a new school, clear information is given about who is who in the school, what their roles are and who to go to if support is needed.

Once the professional relationship is established, then a 'working relationship' will begin to develop. A working relationship still has the fundamental core elements of the professional relationship but becomes deeper and more trust is developed. The working relationship comes from a deeper understanding of each other and involves a greater connection. From the working relationship, a 'friendly relationship' can be developed. The friendly relationship is established from repeated connections, a more in-depth understanding of each party and a deeper connection. It is often co-created by both parties as they feel more secure in the relationship. There is a freer and more flexible connection, but it still has a clear set of boundaries.

Real-life example (Sonia)

When asked to go into a school to undertake some direct work with Sahid, he was initially reluctant to engage with me. He had his arms folded and head down, reluctant to speak. At this point, he did not know who I was and what I was going to do. Firstly, I had to establish a professional relationship by introducing myself, explaining my role and informing him that his parents and teachers had asked me to see him, because sometimes his big feelings took over. Following this, I explained that we would be meeting on a weekly basis and that we would undertake some playful activities to help him learn to manage his emotions. To develop the sense of safety, we agreed on some boundaries that would help us to feel safe.

By turning up and fulfilling the activities discussed and agreed in the professional stage, the relationship began to develop into a working one. We got to know each other. I learnt that he liked reading Harry Potter books, so we began to use different playful activities about Harry Potter and how Harry managed his big feelings. Sahid began to enjoy our times; however, this led to him wanting more time and being reluctant to leave our sessions. This is where the clear boundaries identified in the professional relationship came in, as I was able to remind him of the ending time of our session. He pushed the boundaries for a couple of sessions, but with my persistent enforcement of the time boundary, he began to accept it based on his trust in the relationship.

Towards the end of our planned sessions, our relationship had developed into a friendly relationship. We had become comfortable with each other; the relationship felt freer, and we were able to make jokes and laugh together. Due to the clarity at the beginning of the relationship about the number of sessions we had together, Sahid was able to accept working through the ending of the relationship. We were both able to acknowledge the relationship process and the development of his emotional regulation. The relationship enabled him to risk exploring his big feelings and to find different ways of managing them.

The clarity of role and understood boundaries are essential in developing a good working relationship that will support identified outcomes. We are reminded of a child who established a deep, friendly relationship with their one-to-one key adult, but unfortunately a clear outline of the key adult's role had not been given to the pupil. When it was time for the pupil to move to another school, they were furious that the one-to-one key adult was not moving with them. They had believed that this person would always be with them. They felt let down, rejected and abandoned. Careful work needed to be undertaken to work through this belief and help the pupil move to their next provision

Professional

- creates safety in the relationship
- delineates the role
- clarifies the boundaries

Working

- slightly deeper
- developing a way of working together

Friendly

- more in-depth relationship but not the person's best friend
- co-created relationship developed from a deeper understanding of each other

Reflection Point

Think of the pupils in your setting and analyse the type of relationships you have with them.

The relationships between staff and pupils in the learning environment will be most effective when developed in a careful and appropriate order: from professional, progressing to working, moving on to friendly. These relationship stages will help establish and embed systems, routines, strategies and interventions, though the process is not as sequenced as this notion may suggest. The staff do not develop these relationship stages in isolation, it works alongside the teacher establishing the structure, the routine and portraying their confident presence. However, it is important not to diminish the importance of relationships as providing the foundations for productive learning in the environment. These relationships will determine the effectiveness of all that follows: the routines, the boundaries, the expectations, the behaviour plan, strategies and interventions. Without secure relationships between staff and pupils in the classroom, their effectiveness will be limited. If staff do not develop and maintain relationships with their pupils, then the management of behaviour becomes merely a process of implementing techniques to establish control of the learning environment. There may be control through the force of personality of the staff but take that away and we are left with a learning environment that does not have a clear structure that is understood by all and an environment of uncertainty. This could be the reason for a child, group or class behaving entirely differently for different staff.

Attachment theory and the learning environment

When thinking about the development of relationships in the learning environment, there needs to be some appreciation of attachment theory. It has taken on greater significance in schools in recent years. It is important for educators to have an understanding of attachment theory, as attachment can influence the child's ability to develop relationships with others. It is becoming widely referred to and more educators are becoming 'attachment aware'. Theories of attachment provide a helpful framework for understanding some behaviours and has put the importance of relationships in school back on the agenda.

Attachment theory is about the early relationship that the child develops with their primary caregiver and is a survival strategy. This first relationship has a major influence on the child's perception of relationships and their view of the world. In other words, it is the blueprint for all other relationships. Our attachment systems are how we make sense of relationships (family and friends) and how this internally makes us feel (safe and secure/happy or anxious/unhappy). Attachment typically takes place from birth to one year of age; however, attachment lasts a lifetime and is continually being reinforced or adapted. Secure attachment relationships enable the child to develop an internalised sense of safety and security; they learn to regulate their emotions and behavioural response by their primary caregiver soothing their distress, creating joy, supporting a calm state and providing a secure base from which to explore. The trust and safety that is developed from a secure attachment is the foundation stage of child development.

Humans are driven to make relationships in order to survive; pupils learn about how to function in relationships initially from their caregivers. By receiving consistent, predictable, positive serve-and-return interactions, pupils develop skills to form and maintain healthy relationships and perceive caregivers/ adults as trustworthy sources of comfort and support. Babies 'serve' by making a noise or movement, the adult 'returns' with a sensitive and attuned response (Center on the Developing Child at Harvard University, 2017). Attuned return responses enable the child to develop emotional and behavioural regulation, and neuro-networks, particularly executive functioning skills in the prefrontal cortex, are built (Murray, 2017). With these regular and consistent attuned responses, it takes a newborn baby approximately nine months to develop a secure attachment. However, if the baby does not receive these, they may develop insecure attachments. There are three different styles of insecure attachment:

- insecure avoidant
- insecure ambivalent/dismissive
- disorganised.

This presents a number of challenges for educators, as contrasting strategies are needed for the different insecure attachment styles. A detailed discussion of attachment theory is beyond the scope of this book; for more information on attachment, please see the References on pp152-5.

Insecure attachment and the learning environment

All pupils need relationships with others, but some may need support in learning how to develop them. Most pupils will have developed the ability to form and sustain relationships by the time they start school. They will have experienced consistent, calm and regulating care from their caregivers, which has enabled them to have an internalised perception that relationships are safe and grown-ups will endeavour to help them. Therefore, when educators connect with them and provide support, they engage in the relationship and accept the help. However, some pupils may enter school with an internalised view that relationships are harmful and unsafe, or with an inability to create and maintain attachments. They may have developed insecure early attachment relationships and may have an internal perception that adults will not help them or may be damaging. So, the well-intentioned actions by a teacher may be perceived as a threat.

Reflection Point

Thinking about Jimmy, his experiences of relationships were of being neglected, physically hurt, rejected and negated. Therefore, he brought his internalised experiences to every connection with school staff and peers. His perception, almost an expectation, was that the teachers would physically and/or emotionally hurt him. Therefore, he used protective survival behaviours to keep them at a distance. Once the teaching staff understood his survival strategies, they were able to gently model, explain and teach him that some relationships are safe, and he could risk connecting with them. It took time and lots of repetition.

The biggest challenges for establishing relationships tend to occur in secondary schools. The structure of the timetable, the pressure of the curriculum and the need to deliver on the achievement agenda, as defined by current policy, may affect or limit the opportunities for meaningful relationships to be developed. While the role of the adult and child relationship changes as the pupils develop, the fundamental drive to be in connection with another does not. Adolescents need the security of relationships just as much as a younger child. It is interesting that during one of the most challenging stages of child development, the current demands on all in secondary education reduces the opportunities to develop meaningful relationships. There is an emphasis on the importance of the teacher-child relationship in early years, primary and further education, but it is limited in secondary. In further education, the pupils are allocated a personal tutor who will support them with their learning. Unfortunately, in secondary provisions, tutor times have been reduced, therefore limiting the time to build relationships.

In any setting in which relationships are necessary, there are some people we will connect better with than others. This is the case in the teacher–child, teacher–teacher, teacher–teaching assistant and teacher–parent relationship. However, it is the reflective teacher that recognises this within themselves and attempts to understand what is driving the disconnection. Once we understand the cause, we are then able to explore options to address it. The reflective teacher will consider whether it is about themselves, about the child, the co-created interactions or other external influences, such as the drive for academic achievement, successful test results, Ofsted requirements and/or parents.

When considering themselves, there are a whole host of factors that may influence the teacher's potential disconnection. Here are a few:

- Does the child remind them of a previous child?
- Does the child generate a fear response in the teacher?
- Are the strategies the teacher is using inappropriate with this child and the teacher feels inadequate in some way?
- Is there a push for academic achievement?
- Are others making judgements of the child's behaviour and this makes them question their current approach with the child?
- Does the academy trust or school have a particular approach that does not meet the child's need, but that the teacher is required to implement anyway?
- Are there any external factors in the teacher's own experiences that may be influencing the perception of the relationship?

When pondering the child, there are similar questions and views to consider. For instance, in the case of Jimmy, he was using challenging behaviour to protect himself from connecting with the teacher. It may be that the child is struggling to understand physics, so they resist connecting with the physics teacher, because it is safer than looking foolish in front of their peers because they do not understand the learning. It could be that the teacher reminds the child of someone from their past. It may be that they are being influenced about the teacher by others. For example, if the child's parents feel that the teacher is not fulfilling their role in some way, they articulate this in front of the child, who then internalises this view of the teacher.

Reflection Point

Identify the pupils that present you with more challenges in forming relationships with them. Reflect on what might be driving this and how you can manage it.

With this reflection and understanding of the feelings and the underlying driving needs, you can then work at identifying strategies to address the disconnection. Teachers have a duty to attempt to connect with all their pupils and ensure that each and every one of them feels valued while in the educators' care. There will always be some pupils who get deeper into our hearts and are easy to connect with, and some that require more effort and are more difficult to connect with. However, it is the teacher's professional duty of care to establish a connection with all the pupils in the learning environment.

Reflection Point

1. Think about the teachers who were significant to your learning.

- What was it about them and their actions that made a difference?
- What emotions did they and their actions evoke in you?
- What was it about the relationship that was important?
- How can you replicate this with the pupils in your care?

2. Think about the different relationships that you have in the school setting and identify the different forms of relationships.

- Who do you have the professional relationship with?
- Which people do you have working relationships with and who do you have friendly relationships with?

3. Consider how you approach a new class group or individual child.

- How will you establish meaningful relationships?
- What will those pupils need from you to develop a sense of safety in the relationship?

For some pupils, consideration will need to be given to developing their relationship skills. A specific relational development plan could be identified, with strategies and interventions to implement the plan. One strategy could be for a key attachment-aware adult to work directly with the child, or for a team of adults to provide consistent, persistent relational interactions.

Learning Points

- Humans are wired for connections.
- Relationships are one of the core foundation blocks for behaviour support.
- Behaviour exists within the context of relationships.
- Understanding attachment theory is an essential requirement for educators.
- It is crucial to explore the potential disconnections in relationships.

CHAPTER 3

Understanding Behaviour and its Influences

> *'Fear is the path to the dark side. Fear leads to anger. Anger leads to hate. Hate leads to suffering.'*
> Master Yoda in *The Phantom Menace* (released 1999)

Steven was found sitting on top of the basketball hoop, refusing to come down. He had previously run out of class, screeched down the corridor and was shouting and swearing at anyone he passed. These were his typical behavioural reactions to any challenges in the learning environment.

Separately, James was sitting at his desk, putting his hand up and asking for help as he was struggling to understand a maths activity. These were his typical reactions to any challenges in the learning.

Both are examples of behaviours at different points on a spectrum. At one end are behaviours that are considered appropriate and acceptable while, at the other end, the behaviours are deemed inappropriate and antisocial. When we hear the word 'behaviour', particularly if it is applied to pupils, and especially in the context of an education setting, our thoughts are immediately of inappropriate behaviours that impact negatively on a learning environment in general, and on the learning of individuals within that environment. In reality, the majority of behaviours displayed in schools are appropriate and demonstrate the pupils' motivation and voluntary engagement in the learning environment. However, most adults involved in a professional or personal capacity will mostly understand the word 'behaviour' from a negative viewpoint.

When delivering training, we have asked the participants on countless occasions to list behaviours they have experienced in the last month. We rarely get asked if we mean inappropriate or appropriate behaviour and lists are usually, with some exceptions, of inappropriate behaviours. This should not be a surprise, however, as any professional who has worked in a school will know that even a small amount of inappropriate behaviour can command the agenda in a learning environment. The behaviour can lack intensity but occur on a regular basis or it can be intensive but occur infrequently. Whatever the context, it can set the atmosphere of the environment and dictate how participants perceive that environment and interact with it. Having visited, observed and taught in a lot of different learning environments, we have experienced many instances of appropriate behaviour sometimes getting lost in the fog of a limited number of inappropriate behaviours.

The Oxford Learner's Dictionaries (2022) defines behaviour as 'the way in which one acts or conducts oneself, especially towards others,' or 'the way in which an animal or person behaves in response to a particular situation or stimulus'. If behaviour is defined by how we 'act or conduct' ourselves, is this not what a pupil does in a learning environment – engaging, interacting and responding in different situations? When doing these things appropriately, they can be viewed as displaying the appropriate behaviour. However, some pupils and young people may find it difficult to act and conduct themselves appropriately. They may have learnt other behaviours when responding in different situations, for a variety of reasons; these will be explored later. These behaviours are at odds with and different from the majority. They are inappropriate behaviours and can impact not only on their own learning and wellbeing, but on the learning and wellbeing of others.

Children are not born knowing how to behave in situations; it is a learnt skill and requires empathic, consistent, predictable, patient and persistent guidance to enable it to grow, develop and become embedded as the norm. However, this can be at odds with a general belief that pupils should know how to behave. Often it is perceived that they are consciously and purposely undertaking inappropriate behaviours, therefore they can control them. This view fails to consider that they are pupils and are on a developmental trajectory that is not fully mature until they are into their early twenties. Society often has higher expectations of pupils and is sometimes more critical of pupils' behaviour than of adults engaged in the same behaviours. Cotton (2017) describes asking teachers how they would respond if a pupil angrily knocked over a chair in their classroom. They reportedly responded by telling the pupil to leave the class or to pick up the chair. He then asks how they would respond if one of their colleagues walked into the staffroom and angrily threw over a chair. Many state that they would ask their colleague what had happened or if they are alright; they would then pick up the chair for them. He posits that, with pupils, we tend to only see the presenting behaviours and do not explore the underlying root of the behaviour, but with adults we are more likely to look for reasons beneath the surface. Why is it that we are more tolerant of adults, who have adult behavioural regulation and mature brains, than we are of pupils, who are only just developing their regulation skills and have underdeveloped prefrontal cortices (the area of the brain that helps to manage emotional and behavioural responses)?

Reflection Point

Consider your initial responses to the following situations:

James, aged 11, throws his book across the desk.	Tom, aged 43, throws his book across the desk.
Lucy, aged 9, needs to go to the toilet in the middle of the lesson.	Jenny, aged 39, needs to go to the toilet in the middle of a staff meeting.
Ahmed, aged 15, comes to school without a pen.	Hussain, aged 27, comes to staff training without a pen.
Ruth, aged 6, talks to her friend when she is getting her work out, but the class has been told to get their work out silently.	Sarah, aged 51, talks to her colleague while preparing for an activity during a training course.
Richard, aged 13, runs down the corridor to get to his next class as he has been held up in his previous lesson.	Adam, aged 31, runs down the corridor to get to his next lesson as he has been held up in a head of year meeting.

With this in mind, we also need to consider that behaviours come from two points: the first being a survival instinctive response (the need to feel safe) and the second being a cognitive thoughtful intent. It is necessary for educators to understand the differences, as one is a body-and-brain survival instinctive response to threat and the other is a thought-through action. The younger the child, the more likely the behaviours are coming from a survival instinctive response than a cognitive point, as their prefrontal cortex (the thinking part of the brain) is only just developing. Additionally, if the pupil has special educational needs or has experienced traumatic life experiences, they may not have had opportunities to learn the regulatory skills needed to manage the survival instinctive responses. This will be discussed in greater length in Chapter 6. In a class of 30 pupils, no matter what the year group, there will be a range of behavioural regulation abilities.

Delahook (2019) defines behaviour as 'the observable response to our internal and external experiences … behaviours are outward manifestations of a person's internal bodily processes, perceptions, emotions, thoughts and intentions' (p.15). This would suggest behaviour is a form of communication. If we accept this definition of behaviour, we can then understand the child's or young person's actions as a way of trying to tell us something. It would be easy if pupils were able to articulate their feelings about and emotional responses to a situation, but this requires high-level cognitive thinking, which is only developed later in childhood. If Steven had been able to articulate that he was terrified of getting the maths equation wrong and was feeling like a failure, he may not have needed to behaviourally communicate this by climbing to the top of the basketball hoop. However, the perception or understanding of what is being communicated by another through their behaviour is not straightforward. Think about the pupil who is given three simple instructions (from the teacher's point of view): 'Go to the cupboard, get your book and take it back to your seat.' At the point of walking to the cupboard, the pupil wanders around, distracting others and takes an age to complete the three instructions, if at all. On first observation, it may seem the child is being non-compliant or defiant. However, it could be viewed from several different perspectives. It could be that the pupil may be feeling anxious about the activity and engaging in these behaviours to protect themselves. Or they may have misheard the instruction or interpreted it differently from what the teacher expected – there may be processing issues or other issues around cognitive development. It may be that they just do not want to do it. By defining and understanding the underlying need or drive for the specific behaviour, we will determine a different response.

A response or strategy based merely on the observed behaviours will provide only one element of the information needed to meaningfully respond and manage the behaviour. We need to look beyond the initial behaviour and explore underlying roots, as this will help provide a more holistic approach to support. When the inappropriate behaviour of a pupil is not understood, or the perception of what the behaviour means is incorrect, it may leave all parties feeling confused and unsure how to respond. A confused response may lead to frustration and more inappropriate behaviours. Therefore, understanding what the pupil is trying to communicate with their behaviours is vital if we want to change an inappropriate behaviour into an appropriate one. It will also stop the 'blame game': too often pupils in school can be blamed for their behaviour, which leads to a response of consequence and punishment as the initial way of trying to change it.

Understanding behaviour

To begin to understand what is being communicated through the behaviour, we first must look at or try to discover what may have influenced or initiated the behaviour. Behaviour can be influenced by many things, and these can include issues such as:

- inconsistent or limited experiences of nurture
- lack of consistent, supportive parental care
- feeling unloved
- adults' emotional and behavioural regulation
- fear

- pain
- attachment issues
- traumatic experiences
- bullying
- poverty
- the environment in the school, home or community
- different types of abuse
- parental issues, including parental knowledge, mental and/or physical health difficulties
- unidentified physical, emotional and/or learning needs
- communication issues
- loss
- bereavement
- medical issues
- anxiety.

This list could be endless as there are many factors that can influence a pupil's behavioural responses.

Reflection Point

Take a few moments to think about a pupil in your care and consider the factors that may be influencing their behaviours.

One of the drivers for any behaviour is the desire to meet an underlying need. This need may not even be fully understood by the child; however, a fundamental part of the adult's role is to identify this driver. In order to change an inappropriate behaviour, it is essential that we understand the driving need, even if this was triggered a long time ago and the behaviour has become the pupil's usual or learnt way to respond. In addressing behaviour, firstly we need to unpeel it and look beneath the presenting action to uncover the root need or cause.

One useful analogy is of an apple tree in autumn. The apples are ready for harvesting, but the tree has only fulfilled its potential through a number of factors and influences. This begins with the initial germination of the seed in well-fertilised soil, with enough space to expand and grow. When the roots of the tree are established and strong, the tree is tended and cared for, watered, fed, even pruned when necessary. There are other supporting factors, such as protection against insects, slugs, birds and the weather. All these elements produce the apple. Some are obvious, some are hidden, some can only succeed if others are provided (for example, you can plant in the best soil but if you don't water there will be no apples).

Apple trees need...	Children need...
planting on higher ground, not too close to streams or woods, as these are harmful to apple trees	a safe and nurturing environment, and not to be exposed to limiting or harmful factors
space for the root ball to grow and expand, otherwise the tree is stunted	a creative and motivating environment that stimulates the thirst for learning varied, challenging and positive opportunities
well-fertilised soil	a creative and motivating environment that stimulates the thirst for learning
lots of sunlight and appropriate amounts of rain	positive and regular attention
regular pruning at the right time	clear and consistent boundaries
regular watering	a healthy diet
staking of the tree to support growth, as and when needed	predictable, persistent, consistent nurturing support
protection from slugs, insects and birds	secure attachments and relationships
space to grow	encouragement and guidance
a gardener who will tend to the tree's needs	adults to contain and scaffold, support, manage and contain emotional responses and behaviour help to develop emotional and behavioural self-regulation adults around them with strong emotional and behavioural regulation

Apple trees need...	Children need...
cross-pollination	opportunities to interact with other children, adults, animals, situations and environments
cold weather, to allow the tree to rest and prepare for the production of blossom needed for apples to grow.	opportunities to sleep, rest, relax and recuperate

The development of positive and productive behaviours is a process that requires nurture, support, guidance, time and a consistent environment that is predictable and has clear boundaries. But, as with a fruit, we are persuaded to see the behaviour as limited to the end product, disconnected from what has caused it; therefore, we only react to the behaviour itself rather than responding to an identified need.

The Fruit = The Presenting Behaviours

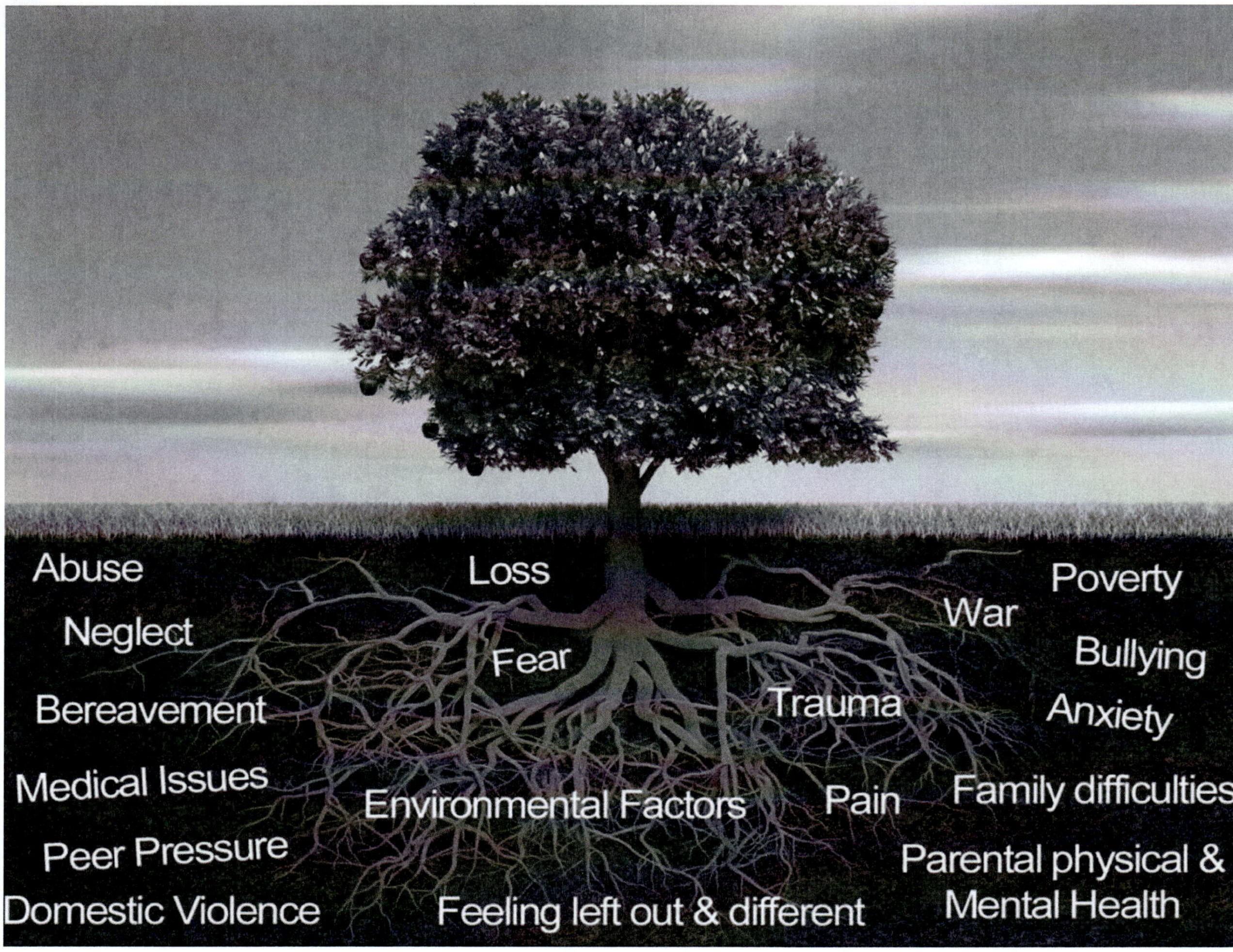

(Orlando Florin Rosu, Adobe Stock)

The Roots = The Underlying Causes of Inappropriate Behaviour

We need to look beneath the fruit to the root cause. Looking beyond what is presented enables the practitioner to have a clearer understanding of what is causing the behaviour; once we have a clearer understanding, we can develop appropriate strategies to support the behaviour. Most pupils do not want to behave in inappropriate ways; it is either caused by their survival instinctive responses or they have learnt these strategies, which have become tied to their drivers to meet an underlying unmet need. As Oaklander (1988, p.205), states:

> 'I do not view a child's behaviour, displeasing as it may sometimes be, as sickness. I view it as the child's evidence of strength and survival. A child will do what he can in any way to survive in this world. He will do what he thinks is the best thing to do to get through the job of growing up.'

This quote has been our mantra since the early 1990s and is the premise by which we develop our responses to behaviour. It shifts the view of behaviour from a negative perspective to looking at it from a strengths-based view: one that views behaviour as the way the pupil is using adaptive responses to manage situations.

There are a whole range of factors that could be the root cause or causes of the behaviours. It may be only one element or it may be a combination of factors. Real-life examples: a child may experience doing poorly in a test and believe that they can never succeed in that subject; they may have experienced a one-off traumatic event, such as a car accident or their house being struck by lightning, which might influence their behaviours; for others, they may have experienced a range of events and for enduring lengths of time.

If a behaviour (the fruit) is driven by an unmet need, the pupil may experience a level of anxiety (the root) and communicate that through their behaviour. If the response to the behaviour is based on a lack of understanding or appreciation of the behaviour, it can become an entrenched learnt response. Behaviours take on a protective nature as a way of keeping the child safe and are driven by the fear of not being safe. This does not completely replace the influences of other factors but, in certain circumstances, fear can be one of the most significant driving causes of an inappropriate behaviour.

According to Forbes & Post (2006), fear and the need for safety are the underlying causes for most behaviours initially, but are often disguised as other emotions. Children have the same emotional responses as adults but, due to their developing brains, they often do not have the understanding to recognise them or the language development to articulate them. Fear is essential to protect ourselves from potential threat and danger. It is an adaptive and often instantaneous reaction to ensure survival. When babies are born, their brains are underdeveloped; they are functioning from the limbic part of their brain (emotional brain) and the brain stem (survival brain). Both these elements of the brain are designed to detect any threat and ensure survival.

The polyvagal theory (Porges, 2011) provides further understanding of pupils' fear-related behaviours. The human body's nervous system is wired to assess for threat and move the body to safety. Porges ascertained three neurophysiological states: social engagement (ventral vagal nerve), defence (fight or flight response from the sympathetic nerve) or life threat (freeze and shutdown response from the parasympathetic nerve). A child's body and brain will react instinctively to the perceived threat. They will cry to get their adult to protect them, move their limbs and/or their body to retreat from the threat (defence state) or automatically hold themselves still if they are unable to get away from the threat (life threat state). If the baby is soothed when they are frightened, they and their bodies quickly return to the social engagement state and they feel safe, then their brains and bodies are ready to engage, explore and learn.

Therefore, in the first few months of life, the baby's behaviours are based on an instinctive survival response. How they learn to develop the regulatory skills to override their survival reactions and manage their emotions later in life depends on how these fears are supported by the adults around them in their first few years of life. Murray (2020) notes that pupils 'require repeated nurturing experiences to build the neurological networks between the prefrontal cortex and the brain stem to regulate and override survival reactions' (p.156). A caregiver who soothes and calms a baby when they become frightened and distressed reduces the emotional response in the short term, but if the caregiver repeats these actions, the baby begins to develop their own regulatory skills. Self-regulation can only develop following being regulated by another person. As noted by Wilson *et al.* (1990), secure attachment facilitates the transfer of regulatory skills from caregiver to child. Self-regulation incorporates affect (emotion) regulation and behavioural regulation, both of which are necessary elements to function within groups and the school setting.

However, at any point, when we feel under threat, the nervous system and the brain will take over and do what it needs to do to ensure safety. If we think again about Steven, his early life experiences were of neglect, often being left in a frightened state with no adult to soothe and calm him; therefore, he did not learn how to regulate his emotional states. His brain and body took over in the maths lesson and his nervous system made him flee the threat and find a place of safety. He had climbed to the highest point in the school to ensure his own safety. From that viewpoint, he could scan the whole environment and identify any potential threat. To us, it was a place of threat but, to him, it was a place of safety. Only from there was he able to begin to calm. Unfortunately, due to his life experiences, his body and brain were rarely in the calm social engagement state, and this made the learning environment very challenging for him. His hypervigilant state ensured that his body was constantly on the lookout for real or perceived threat. He was unable to take in any of the learning.

To learn anything, humans have to feel safe (Porges, 2011). If they are feeling in danger or frightened, their brains and bodies will be spending all their energies on ensuring their safety. Therefore, it is imperative when dealing with behavioural challenges to look at whether all parties are feeling safe. If the teacher is not feeling secure, their brains and bodies will be reacting to that and conveying it to all around them. This is the same for the child. Our first priority, then, is to ensure they feel safe. Learning can only take place when everyone feels safe.

Real-life example

Calum, aged four, was starting school. He had been taking his older brother to school for two years and had met his teacher on transition day. (However, that was two months previously.) He was one of three pupils starting that day as the school did a staggered intake. Staggered intakes are a great idea, in theory, as the teacher can focus wholly on the few pupils starting that day. They can connect and begin building the relationship necessary to convey that school is safe. However, to establish the relationship, it is suggested that the new pupils should come in at 8.30am, before everyone else, and that time is spent helping them to feel safe. Unfortunately, this was not the case for Calum. On the morning he started school, he skipped into his class and eagerly explored the room with his parent. The room was full of parents and the teaching staff were busy. At no point was Calum welcomed to the class by his teaching staff. Other than his parent, nobody communicated to him that school was safe and that everything was going to remain safe. He was playing happily on the whiteboard and, at this point, the parents were asked to leave. Still none of the teaching staff had connected with him.

His parent gave him a kiss and explained that it was time for them to leave. Calum waved and turned back to the whiteboard. However, by the time his parent had reached the door, he was running across the room, crying and trying to get to his parent. At this point, one of the teaching staff intervened and attempted to contain him. He then started thrashing about, trying to get to his parent. He was not hitting the staff member on purpose; he was responding from a survival instinctive response. She was a threat to him as he did not know her, and she was stopping him from getting to his place of safety – his parent. His parent soothed and calmed him.

At this point, his teacher began to connect with him. Unfortunately, it was too late – the initial experience developed the perception that school was unsafe. The teaching staff had not portrayed confidence that school was safe. For the next two full terms, Calum cried every morning and every evening about not wanting to go to school. He started biting his nails, was reluctant to leave his parents' sides and became generally unsettled. The saddest part of this experience is that he entered Year 1 on an Individual Education Plan (IEP) for his learning (along with a high proportion of his class peers). He had been able to write his name when he left preschool but, by the end of reception, he could no longer do this. Unfortunately, his learning had been impaired because he physically and psychologically felt unsafe in school. Thankfully, he had a strong, confident teacher in Year 1 who generated safety in her classroom and he quickly caught up.

Educators are		Pupils feel		They are
P = Predictable **C** = Consistent **P** = Persistent **C** = Confident **P** = Patient **C** = Compassionate	=	• A sense of safety • Connected • A sense of predictability • Confident • Reassured	=	**Able to learn**

Although 'infants are born with a limited number of innate fears and these are linked to the drive for survival, of which, the main fears are loud noises and of falling' (Murray, 2020, p.156), their personal experiences and brain development mean that, by the time pupils have reached school age, they may have developed more anxieties. It is therefore useful to explore some of the fears that pupils and young people may experience in and out of school.

- being physically hurt
- getting it wrong
- letting people down
- not being clever enough
- not being loved
- being left out
- not belonging
- being rejected
- being laughed at
- failing
- not having any friends
- being abandoned

Reflection Point

Think about a pupil you are working with and identify some of their potential fears.

The list can go on; however, the ultimate fear beneath the majority of these concerns is the fear of not surviving. Although this might seem far-fetched in a school context, 'survival' is linked to the things we need to thrive, such as acceptance from our social group, the ability to learn skills, achieving independence and so on. If these necessities seem out of reach or threatened, the resulting fear response can be extreme. For instance, the pupil who refuses to put pen to paper may be driven by the fear of failure, getting it wrong or being rejected. We are genetically programmed to try and survive, and any potential threat to our survival will trigger a fear-based behaviour. Some fears are more prevalent at different developmental ages; for example, the need to belong to a peer group is highly significant for most adolescents, but not quite as important to a three-year-old.

Often fear is the primary emotional response, then secondary feelings take over and behavioural responses develop. Real-life example: a child is bitten by a dog; the primary emotion is fear as the experience poses a potential threat to their survival, but then a secondary feeling of anxiety develops as the child worries that they may get bitten again. They then develop behaviour responses to deal with that anxiety, so every time they see or hear a dog they cry, shake, scream and try to run away.

Transfer this example into a learning environment. A pupil takes part in a whole group maths activity (such as Minute Maths Drills or Maths Mad Minutes, as they are known to many teachers). These are worksheets with simple drill-and-practice basic fact maths problems such as addition, subtraction, division or multiplication. Pupils are given a short period of time (usually three minutes or so) to complete as many problems as they can. Feedback is often immediate, so pupils are aware of how others in the class have performed. A pupil who performs badly or finds the format of the structure difficult to succeed in may well experience secondary feelings of anger and hostility at having to do the activity, or shame and frustration when they try but fail (according to agreed perception); they may feel envious and jealous of peers who succeed and isolated as well.

These feelings are generated by the primary emotion of fear of the activity and this fear is communicated by behaviours anywhere on the spectrum: from simple defiance such as a refusal to join in, more intensive behaviours such as walking away from the activity and out of class, to high-intensity behaviours such as screaming, shouting or aggression aimed at disturbing the lesson to the point that it cannot be delivered.

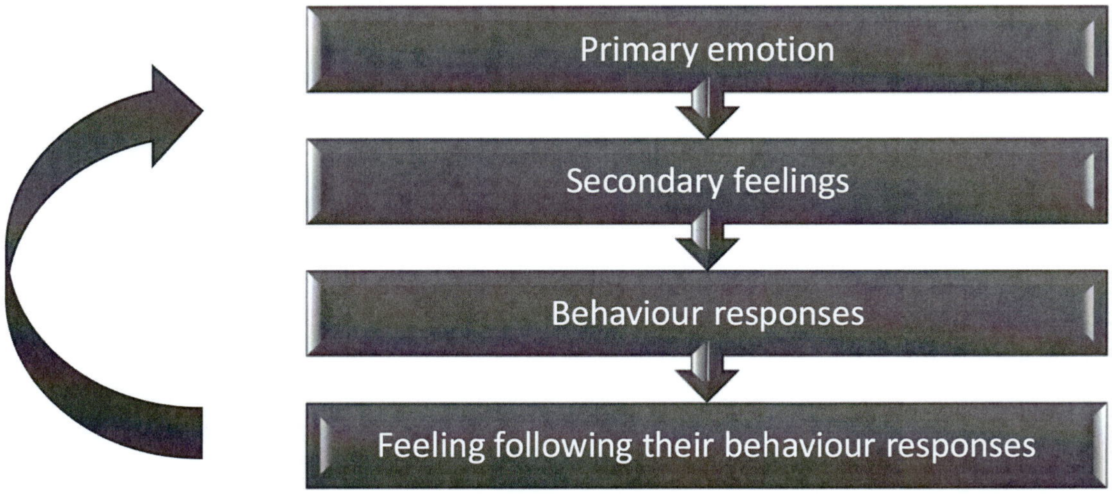

The feeling a child experiences following their behavioural responses can drive them to repeat those behaviours. Real-life example: a pupil may feel relieved when directed out of the classroom as a result of throwing their work across the room, because the other pupils in the class cannot see that they are unable to do the work. The inappropriate behaviour has enabled the pupil to avoid feelings associated with trying and failing at the activity. The pupil learns to cope with fear-based emotions and feelings associated with them by behaving in a socially inappropriate way to protect themselves.

The emotional and behavioural responses of others to the behaviour can also encourage the behaviour to occur again. In the long run, this may also provide a solution, if the behaviour and reason for it are identified and responded to accordingly. Real-life example: a pupil is demonstrating anxiety/fear about an activity at the beginning or before it starts. Worry is beginning to develop in the pupil and is manifested in behaviours such as fidgeting, fiddling, distracting or disengaging. They are communicating, 'I am scared that I can't do it'. If the adult understands the reason or root cause for the behaviour, their response to it will be based on this reasoning and understanding. In this example, support and reassurance will be offered to try and ameliorate the anxiety. However, if the behaviour is misunderstood or missed, the fear/anxiety will grow and may move into secondary emotions such as anger, shame and frustration. Then the pupil's behaviours may move up the spectrum to include banging on the table, shouting across the classroom or walking out. Often, it is at this point we react to the behaviours. Unfortunately, this can lead to the behaviour being repeated, as it becomes a learnt response: the pupil learns that attention is only given when the behaviours have moved along the spectrum. Because the driving need is to gain attention to help minimise the fear, they quickly learn to escalate to prevent living with this overwhelming emotion.

Most pupils, by the age of four, are able to regulate their emotional and behavioural responses the majority of the time. However, it needs to be recognised that these skills will not be fully developed until their mid to late twenties. They will, at times, forget things, become overwhelmed and may react to situations with less tolerance. Unfortunately, by the time they enter school, some pupils will not have learnt the typical regulatory skills and will have learnt to escalate their behaviours to get their needs met. Therefore, they may enter a classroom believing that their needs will not be met and will use protective behaviours to make themselves feel safe. The responses of adults to behaviours in the learning environment will be explored further in Chapter 5.

Identifying many of the presenting behaviours and feelings associated with anxiety/fear-based emotions can be difficult, as they do not always look like anxiety or fear and, therefore, are often misunderstood. Fear and anxiety wear many different masks, as it is often too painful for a person to show these feelings explicitly; 'fear-based feelings' (Forbes & Post, 2006) can look like, for example, defiance, anger, jealousy, confusion, sadness, shame and embarrassment. When we see these 'masks', we tend to react to what we see rather than respond to the underlying, driving fear.

Anxiety/fear-based emotion can change the way we think and feel and, therefore, the behaviour that will follow. The Team Teach model of the conflict spiral (2019, p.36) shows how an experience can shape an emotion or feeling, which drives a behaviour, which then gets a reaction; these behaviours can include shouting, screaming, destroying, fighting, running away, stealing, lying and so on (Forbes & Post, 2006). The following exercise will help to illustrate this.

The alarm has failed to go off and you have woken up late. You need to get to work in under an hour or you will be late for an important meeting. Unfortunately, on that morning, your children are moving at the pace of snails and the traffic is heavier than usual.

Consider your reactions to the experience. Do you look:

- frightened
- anxious
- relaxed and happy
- sad?

Or are you looking:

- stressed
- angry
- furious?

Now think about the underlying feelings. Are you thinking:

- I will be reprimanded by my boss
- I will be humiliated if I get to the meeting late
- If I am not there on time, I will be letting my colleagues down
- My colleagues will think I am unprofessional

Consider your behaviour responses. Are you:

- calmly getting ready?
- talking in a calm voice to your children?
- driving calmly and not becoming agitated with the traffic?

Or are you:

- rushing around, scrabbling to get yourself and your children ready?
- using a raised voice to encourage your children along?
- shouting at the traffic?

This activity demonstrates how, to try to understand behavioural responses to fear-based emotions, we need to put on 'fear x-ray spectacles'. By recognising and understanding an underlying fear, you can then implement appropriate strategies to manage the anxiety and the connected behaviours.

Defining the actual behaviour is often challenging, and we invariably use non-specific and unclear descriptions, such as the pupil is 'having a wobble', 'kicking off' or 'being aggressive'. When trying to manage and change behaviour responses, it is imperative that educators clearly define the behaviour that is presenting some challenges and articulate plainly the desired behaviour. We need to be clear in our descriptions of behaviours, as consideration needs to be given to our pupils' cognitive and language development. If the description is clear, it stops confusion and prevents us focusing on the wrong behaviours. The clarity provides pathways to understanding the underlying root, which in turn helps us to stay in a calm, regulated state when we are trying to manage it.

The description needs to define the actions of the behaviour without offering a value judgement or making assumptions. Often it involves utilising an 'ING' word. Real-life examples: 'Linda was shouting', 'Timmy was tapping the desk with his ruler' and 'Toby was hitting Mark with a stick'. These descriptions are clear and factual. A further discussion will take place in the strategies and interventions section.

Reflection Point

Think about challenging behaviours you have experienced in the learning environment.

List non-specific and unclear behaviour descriptions

Now transfer the above unclear behaviour descriptions into clear and factual behavioural descriptions.

Learning points

- Behaviour comes from two points, a survival response and/or a cognitive thoughtful (thought through) response.
- The importance of looking for the underlying cause (the roots) for the challenging behaviour.
- Consideration to be given to potential fears that might be driving the challenging behaviours.
- Self-regulation can only develop following being regulated by another person initially.
- For learning to take place, a sense of safety needs to be established.

CHAPTER 4

Establishing a Culture That Supports the Behaviour Plan

> *'How wonderful it is that nobody need wait a single moment before starting to improve the world.'*
> Anne Frank

On a visit to a school reception area, we will usually be greeted with a display of various awards and plaques, teachers' pictures and other information such as a mission or vision statement. It is easy to ignore these displays or even be dismissive of them; however, we should take the time to read and look, as they are the first indications of the school's guiding principles. They may be expressed in words such as respect, resilience, determination, inclusion, responsibility, honesty, trust and kindness: core values such as these represent the school culture to the visitor and inform all of the ethos that underpins the practice.

The definition of culture is 'the attitudes, behaviours, opinions, etc. of a particular group of people within society' (Cambridge University Press, 2022b). All learning environments, such as a group, a classroom, department or school, need to have a defined ethos to provide the foundations of all productive learning.

Bennett's (2017) independent review of behaviour in schools emphasises the importance of having a strong culture of behaviour throughout all aspects of the school. He cites consistency, clear expectations, clarity of core values and effective communication as essential components of a positive culture of behaviour. He suggests that a school will develop a culture, whatever the environment, and that it is therefore better if the school takes ownership of this and develops one that encourages good behaviour 'rather than one that impedes it' (Bennett, 2017, p.30).

An effective culture needs to influence practice and develop an environment where appropriate behaviour can thrive. To demonstrate this, a school needs to define what it means by appropriate behaviour. A statement of ethos is useful as guidance, but there needs to be clarity about how this is put into practice.

Reflection Point: Time to think about my practice

- What does the first impression of your school and your class portray to a visitor? (A visitor can be anybody: a child, a parent, an Ofsted inspector or a prospective teacher.)
- Does the reception area reflect the culture and ethos of the school?
- Are the values displayed and are they prominent enough?

The Relationship between Policy, Culture and the Behaviour Plan

The values of a school will reflect its aims and objectives. The outcomes it wants to achieve for its learners determine how policy is implemented. Each school will have its own emphases on learning, behaviour and wellbeing. 'Each school has its own culture and related priorities, which means that the emphasis placed on learning about and working towards emotional well-being can vary considerably' (French & Klein, 2012, p.55).

Reflection Point: Time to think about my practice

- Describe your school's culture and ethos.
- Consider your school's emphases on learning, behaviour and wellbeing.
- How do the school's emphases mirror/differ from your own?

The school's ethos and culture should be more than a mission statement of desired outcomes; it should provide a framework of how teachers will implement the behaviour policy in their learning environments. The word 'policy' refers to 'a set of ideas or a plan of what to do in particular situations that has been agreed to officially by a group of people, a business organisation, a government, or a political party' (Cambridge University Press, 2022c). The strategic and operational direction of policy establishes and gives expression to the culture in the learning environments. The tool used to implement policy is the behaviour plan. By setting out the key elements needed in the learning environment, with clear guidance about how behaviour is to be managed and supported, the behaviour plan provides a practical blueprint for how the school's culture and ethos will be implemented consistently by teachers.

It is important the behaviour plan meets the needs of all pupils, not just a select few or only those who are a cause of concern. It should encourage planned responses rather than knee-jerk reactions to behaviours. It should give the practitioner the tools to respond rather than react to behaviour. A good behaviour plan reduces the risk of firefighting.

Reflection Point: Time to think about my practice

- Do I have a behaviour plan in my learning environment?
- Does it reflect the school behaviour policy?
- Does it support the school culture and ethos?
- How does the behaviour plan support consistent behaviour support?
- Does my behaviour plan have clear rules, rewards and consequences?
- Are the routines, expectations and boundaries clear in my behaviour plan?
- What values underpin my behaviour plan?

Establishing the Behaviour Contract

Having a behaviour plan to support developing responses to behaviour begins with a behaviour contract. The contract between teacher and pupil can provide clarity as to what is expected of the pupil and how the teacher can support them. It also provides the basis from which a relationship between teacher and pupil can grow. A well-developed relationship between teachers and pupils, on an individual and collective basis, will allow for a behaviour contract to be understood and have a greater chance of becoming embedded in the learning environment. The contract is not a written one; we are not advocating a list of 'this is what I'll do, and this is what you will do', presented with all the ceremony of the Magna Carta, ready for signature and displayed for all to see and refer to. This approach, while well meaning, can become a tool for confrontation: "John, you are not fulfilling your side of the contract by distracting Ian!" or "Sarah you agreed in the contract not to do that!" This has the effect of allowing inappropriate rather than appropriate behaviours to dictate the interactions and the agenda. It also portrays the contract as something negative, acting as a point of reference when things go wrong. It is a reminder of the breakdown in a relationship between the pupil and the teacher, rather than something that supports it.

If based on positive interaction and relationships, rather than a written document, the focus of the contract is on the appropriate behaviours expected within the learning environment. While the contract is closely aligned with the rules, it is more than just a set of dos and don'ts to be rewarded when adhered to or sanctioned when broken. It has a direct relationship with the culture and ethos of the learning environment and the behaviour plan. It is culture that is the driver of the contract and encourages both parties to agree to it. Without the contract, we cannot implement the behaviour plan.

The contract should be explicit about what a pupil and teacher should expect from each other in the learning environment. For example, take a learning environment where teachers believe they have a responsibility to listen to the children: a learning environment that has developed an atmosphere and culture whereby the child knows they will be listened to is a learning environment in which the teachers have a right to expect children to listen to others.

If teachers exercise their responsibility to be clear about the boundaries, expectations and rules, they have a right to expect them to be followed. To put it simply, if teachers teach, they have a right to expect children to try their best and engage without disruption to the environment in which that teaching is taking place. This will mean, however, that if teachers do not implement their own responsibilities, they cannot expect children to implement theirs. If a learning environment does not listen to children or is unclear about the rules and expectations, or if teachers are not consistent in their approach and boundaries are confusing, can children be expected to listen, follow rules or engage?

The contract is based on the idea that the child has a right to expect the teacher to fulfil their responsibilities and the teacher has a right to expect the child to fulfil their responsibilities. It is a symbiotic relationship, one cannot exist without the other. If the teacher does not implement their responsibilities and clearly establish boundaries, they are in breach of the contract. Alternatively, if the child does not implement their responsibility, the child is in breach of the contract.

There may be occasions when someone in the learning environment does not conform to the contract. When inappropriate behaviours occur, before looking to a specific strategy, we need to look at the quality of the relationship between teacher and pupil in that learning environment. It is important to ask where the contract has broken down before seeking a resolution, to ensure the focus of the solution is effective. If the adult has not fulfilled their side of the contract, then this is the starting point, and teachers may need support to begin the process of looking at their teaching practice and relationships with the pupil. However, if the adult has established good relationships and fulfilled their side of the contract, and pupil behaviour is still an issue, the solution needs to address why the pupil is not meeting the expectations of behaviour set out in the contract.

Paul Dix (2017) puts relationships at the heart of behaviour management and describes how the adults affect the culture of a school through those relationships. He goes on to explain that it is the culture of a school, not just strategies, techniques or the latest and most popular interventions, that contributes to successfully responding to behaviour, and it is the adults who determine that culture. He states, 'in behaviour management, culture eats strategy for breakfast. With the right culture the strategies become less important'.

However, embedding culture is not a one-off event but an ongoing process that may need tools, techniques, strategies and interventions to continue its development. One of the tools may be the behaviour contract.

An example of a 'behaviour for learning' contract

CHILD'S RIGHT	CHILD'S RESPONSIBILITY
To feel safe	To act in a safe way
To be listened to	To listen to others
To have clear rules, expectations and boundaries	To follow the rules and accept the boundaries
To be respected	To respect others
To have access to a broad, balanced and stimulating curriculum	To engage
To be encouraged	To respond to support
To be challenged	To ask for support appropriately when needed

Teacher's responsibility: To provide a learning environment where the foundations for productive learning are present. This includes a culture of guiding principles such as expectations, boundaries and support.

The contract in itself will not completely determine the correct strategy and intervention to support behaviour. We need more information: in particular, a clear definition of the inappropriate behaviour and, even more important, a clear definition of the appropriate behaviour we want to reinforce. When the behaviour is defined we need to assess what the child is doing. Defining is made easier by having an established relationship, a recognised culture and ethos, a contract and a behaviour plan in the learning environment. All these elements need to be in place for the appropriate strategy to be successful.

Reflection Point: Time to think about my practice

- Do I have a behaviour contract in my learning environment?
- What are its core elements?
- Do the children understand their responsibilities in the contract?
- What are my responsibilities?

The Behaviour Plan: Rules, Rewards and Consequences

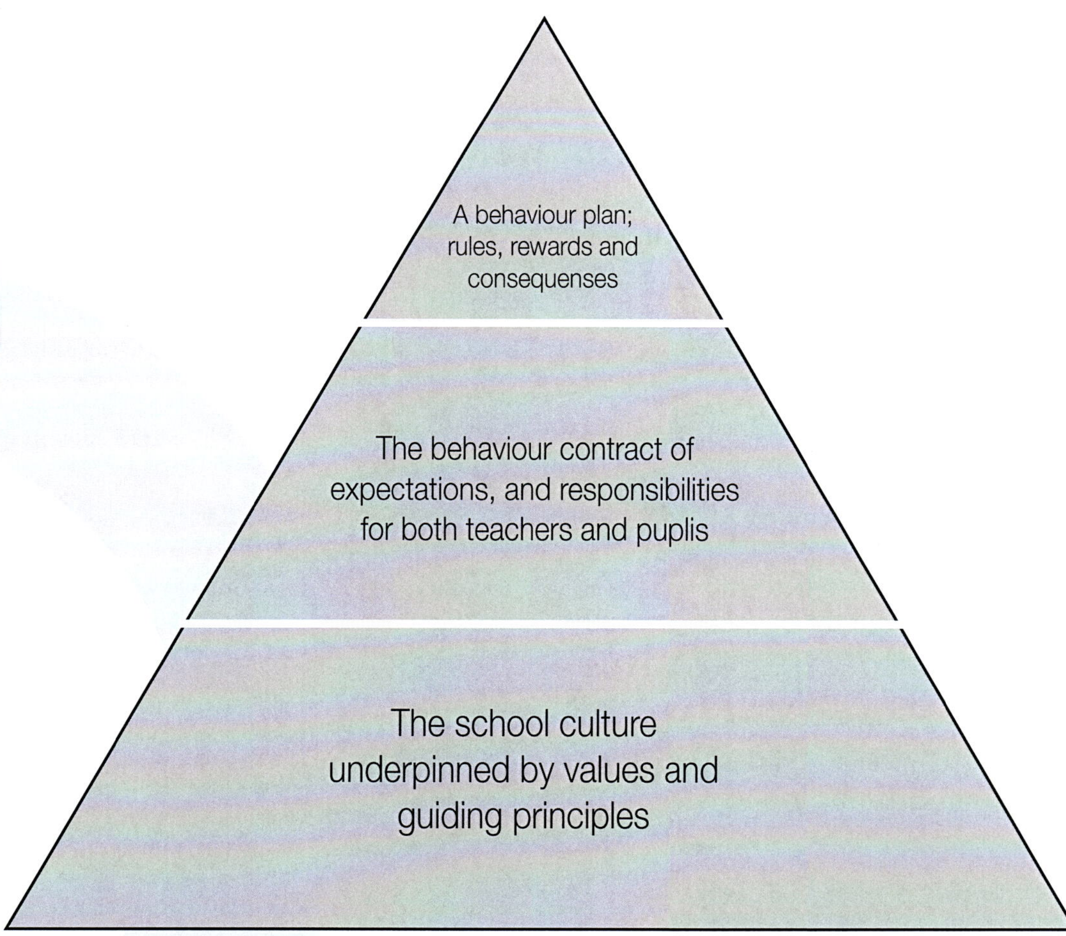

An effective culture will need a robust behaviour plan. The best behaviour plans are usually simple, easy to implement and understood by all. If it is complicated, cumbersome and difficult to use on a day-to-day basis, it will be personalised by teachers who will make slight changes to it to suit the specific needs of their learning environment or department. In a short space of time there will be several plans embedding different cultures and leading to inconsistent practice. As consistency disappears, responses to the same behaviours differ, causing confusion, fragmentation and frustration.

To protect the school and its culture from this fragmentation the plan starts with a set of values that reflect expectations and express an overall aim or vision. They are not rules, they cannot be used as a tool in the same way rules are used in supporting behaviour as they do not have the necessary characteristics. They lack the clarity needed as by definition they are the guiding principles, a starting point from which expectations of desired or appropriate behaviour is determined.

Rules, on the other hand, have the characteristics to manage behaviour; the practical application of the school values, culture and ethos is through the rules, rewards and consequences set out in the behaviour plan. These three elements make it more likely that school staff will develop consistent practice and responses to behaviour.

Rules

The first basic elements of the behaviour plan are the rules. Rules are different to expectations. The expectations will be more aligned to the values, while the rules will provide clarity about how values are implemented.

For example, respect could be an expectation that reflects one of the school's values; it can be implemented by a rule related to a specific behaviour in regard to showing respect. Rules set clear boundaries and limits. They explicitly state the appropriate behaviour expected, they are the tools we use to teach and reinforce expectations. When the appropriate behaviour is exhibited and the expectation met it will need to be re-enforced to motivate the pupil to repeat that behaviour. The rules will need to be specifically taught and constantly referred to. Rules should be taught with the same care any other part of the curriculum would be. Each element of the behaviour plan supports the other two. Appropriate behaviour (following rules and expectations) is rewarded while inappropriate behaviour (not following rules or expectations) has a consequence.

If the rules are intended to support the practical implementation of culture it will be helpful for pupils to not only be informed of the rules and the behaviour plan as a whole, but to make some contribution to its development. The behaviour plan is not an imposed construct handed down by senior leadership, although they will take a leading role in its application. It is also an operational tool and teachers, governors, parents/carers and children should be asked to make a contribution. Asking for a contribution is not negotiating or handing over control.

Rules are not negotiated, a contribution will enable the child to have some sense of ownership and this may increase the possibility of compliance. However, the level of ownership and the contributions made must not compromise the ultimate responsibility teachers have in developing the behaviour plan.

Practical hints for rule setting

1. CLARITY

Rules should describe what the child needs to do. Avoid a list of don'ts; apart from being endless they only focus the attention on the inappropriate behaviour and do not make the appropriate behaviour clear. Rules tell the child what they need to do. Rules must be CLEAR and based on OBSERVABLE behaviours. Be precise, define the appropriate behaviour. Vague rules are difficult to comply with and difficult to enforce.

2. NUMBER

The rules need to be limited in number. As with the list of don'ts, a long list of dos, even if they are clear and descriptive, can be unhelpful. A long list will be cumbersome to refer to and teach. Some rules will become more popular than others and some will get forgotten. Some rules will be implemented more than others, some inappropriate behaviours ignored and some appropriate behaviours will be missed. Children will learn that some rules are more important and some are irrelevant. Use a maximum of five and no less than three. Less than three may make it difficult to cover behaviours in terms of type, context, place and time.

3. TAUGHT

Rules need to be referred to regularly. The rules are the foundations by which we teach behaviour; rules will be constantly referred to, taught and discussed. Do not assume they are known and fully understood in November because they were mentioned at the start of the academic year. The rules will need to be displayed across the school. This will support reference, teaching and discussion. The rules are part of the culture, they give clarity to expected observed behaviours. They are part of the ongoing script used by all teachers all the time. The script can be as simple as, "You need to [behaviour related to rule]".

Remember: Teach the rules with the same care you would any other part of the curriculum.

4. ALWAYS

Rules should apply at all times, they need to be always, same rules in all areas of the school and all day. If we have separate rules for different activities, times of the day or different places it will only get complicated, confusing and difficult to implement. If rules change from classroom to classroom or subject to subject or between teachers then the whole school culture suffers, and consistency of approach cannot be guaranteed. The children's experience of the behaviour plan will be different depending on where they are, who they are with or what they are doing. If this happens a key component of implementation is lost: consistency. Having said that, an effective behaviour plan is dynamic and responsive to need. If a rule needs adaptation due to context make sure the rule is discussed, taught, displayed and do not assume the adaptation is fully understood. It is also important that any adaptation or new rule is introduced to all not some and all areas of the school. Treat the new rule or adaptation like you would any new concept being taught in another part of the curriculum.

Reflection Point: Time to think about my practice

- What are my rules?
- Are they a list of don'ts?
- Are the rules clear?
- Are they rules, expectations or values?
- Are the rules related to behaviour?
- How many rules do I have?
- Are the rules in my learning environment different to rules in other parts of the school?
- How do I teach the rules?
- How do I display the rules?
- Do I have a script to support the rules?

Rewards

Most people are motivated by a reward as a way of acknowledging and recognising something they have done or achieved. We get a reward at the end of the month when we are paid. Rewards support the encouragement of positive behaviour. How we should reward and what type of rewards we use to reinforce appropriate behaviour has and continues to be the subject of much debate.

The debate seems to be about legitimate concerns that reward schemes can actually get in the way or be a barrier to developing good behaviour. The concern centres around the idea that behaviour modification based on reward schemes will not help the child learn to behave for intrinsic reasons but merely to gain the reward. Learning the appropriate behaviour or developing the skills to exhibit the appropriate behaviour for reasons of self-respect, self-worth or personal responsibility are replaced by the selfish need to gain the reward. The process of earning tokens, merits, points, time becomes the focus of attention for the child not the intrinsic need or desire to engage in the appropriate behaviour.

There is also the risk that the administration, recording and monitoring of the reward scheme can become the focus for teachers rather than changing an inappropriate behaviour and teaching an appropriate behaviour. Take away the reward, which is usually tangible, and the child has little motivation in continuing to exhibit an appropriate behaviour. There may be some merit in this view. However, this should not lead us down the path of complete disregard for a scheme that uses tangible rewards. The problems could be an over reliance on tangible rewards and the under usage of non-tangible rewards. It may not be so much about the type of reward used but context, regularity, appropriateness, value and relevancy of the scheme.

Tangible and Non-Tangible Rewards

The first part of the process in any reward structure should be 'catch them being good' and tell them. But do not just tell them they are good, tell them why and how they can continue to exhibit the appropriate behaviour. Positive behaviour should be noticed and acknowledged immediately. It models desired behaviour for other children, reinforces the desired behaviour and encourages the child to continue behaving appropriately. It demonstrates the practical application of expectations and rules and makes them relevant. We may expect children to behave appropriately because it is the 'right' thing to do. However, some may require more tangible reinforcement and motivation.

For example, a child shouting out rather than putting their hand up when they need attention and support may require specific teaching of that behaviour, and a reward may motivate and reinforce the appropriate behaviour. The structure of the reward scheme and the practical implementation of it should be a mixture of both tangible and non-tangible and include both verbal and non-verbal responses. This can include smiley faces, stars, points, earned time to choose an activity. However, and just as importantly, praise, attention, time, smile or a thumbs up.

Initially the primary reinforcer may need to be the tangible reward. If this is the case the tangible reward can be divided into a soft and hard version. The soft version represented by a sticker or name on the wow wall or recognition board, anything that has no actual value or can be 'cashed in' for something else. The hard tangible is represented by a house point or merit where a treat, voucher, time on a chosen activity or certificate can be obtained by a certain number.

At first motivation may need to be rewarded with a hard tangible and with progress replaced with a soft tangible, one where recognition of 'doing the right thing' no longer requires material reward. As the behaviour becomes more embedded the non-tangible will become the primary reinforcer. As the child exhibits the behaviour more and more, and begins to develop their own self-belief and confidence around the behaviour, the need for tangible, particularly hard, rewards may almost become extinct. The child begins to believe they can do it, it feels good to do it and they want to do it, it becomes intrinsic.

Catch them being good

At this point it is easy to fall into the trap of not noticing appropriate behaviour anymore but do not forget to 'catch them being good' periodically as the appropriate behaviour still needs to be reinforced, just with less regularity or intensity. We all like others to notice when we do something well. The child needs to learn that appropriate behaviour is just as likely to get noticed as inappropriate behaviour. Some children may have experienced that the only attention they will get from adults is when they are misbehaving. They learn that inappropriate behaviour is more likely to get a reaction. Positive recognition for appropriate behaviour can break this negative cycle and offer a child an intrinsic non-tangible reward for learning a new, appropriate behaviour. In the long term the positive behaviour will become a reward in itself. Using positive recognition not only encourages children to behave appropriately and to reinforce appropriate behaviour, but it can also increase a child's self-esteem through consistent, meaningful positive recognition. It can let the child know behaviour is noticed, creates a positive learning environment and establish positive relationships.

Remember the children who 'turn up, do and go home'

While some children are not able to sustain appropriate behaviour over a long period and may need immediate recognition and/or reward to motivate and reinforce, there are others who do not need this level of response. It may seem they do not need a reward to re-enforce the behaviour. However, it is important that these children are not forgotten about when it comes to rewarding. In terms of supporting behaviour in the learning environment these children are extremely important. Their behaviour sets the agenda and atmosphere, they are the example of what is expected and they model the behaviour you want all others to notice. It is easy to forget to 'catch them being good.' But it is important we do, not only because it is deserved but by doing so we are showing others a practical demonstration of what the appropriate behaviour looks like.

When our eldest son was in Year 4, on a visit to the class I noticed the reward chart displayed. It was one of those with names horizontal on the left-hand side and stars vertically lined up in front of the name in boxes with a date on. As with all of these type of displayed rewards schemes it is obvious who has the most and who the least. It did make me think of the value of this kind of display. I wondered if we are constantly compared to our peers would we feel enthusiastic or indifferent, motivated or uninspired? I noticed my son had not won a star for over a week and asked the teacher if there was a problem and if so, what I could do to help. At this point the teacher was a little surprised and told me not only was there not a problem but he comes into school every day, follows instructions, does what he's told and follows the routines without any problems. So, I asked why he hadn't got a star on the chart for that week. There was no problem only the fact that he was a 'turn up, do and go home'.

These are the children who 'Turn Up, Do what is expected and Go Home'. They are the children who silently get on because they intrinsically can and want to do it. It is very important not to forget them. Rewarding of any kind should include all, no group will be forgotten. If a group or individual is forgotten, then the reward scheme may seem irrelevant and inadvertently demotivate.

The three elements of the behaviour plan only succeed when the relationship with the other two is explicit. All children need to believe in the plan and therefore it must be demonstrated that by following the rules, by exhibiting the appropriate behaviour, you get a reward. This could just as easily be a non-tangible verbal recognition, or it could be for sustained and continued demonstrations of following the rules you get a tangible, soft or hard. There are many different examples of schemes and ways to reward children. In our experience using both tangible and non-tangible rewards has the best chance of reinforcing appropriate behaviour. Whatever system of rewards you use the following criteria may be useful.

Practical hints for implementing rewards

1. Mix it up

It is always useful to have a mixture of both tangible and non-tangible. Notwithstanding the reasons given earlier children will get bored with the same certificate, voucher, point, smiley face or script over time. The same phrase or way of recognising appropriate behaviour can begin to feel formulaic and sound insincere.

2. Verbal and Non-Verbal

Use verbal and non-verbal means of communication to reward and recognise appropriate behaviour. Sometimes a smile, a thumbs up, a quiet word, a light touch on the shoulder, a wink, a clap, a high five or a handshake can be sufficient. Verbal rewarding may not be as straightforward as expected. Giving praise can be a powerful and effective way of giving positive recognition. Effective praise is personal, genuine, descriptive and specific. It needs to acknowledge and link to the effort as much as the outcome of an activity. The praise may be ineffective or demotivating if it is always based on evaluating (how good you are at something, dependent on outcome) or comparative (compares a child to another), and some children will prefer private praise and find public praise uncomfortable. We need to be specific about the use of praise and what effective praise is. (Driscoll, 1989) states 'Praise is given… when a task or deed is completed or is well done. Encouragement (effective praise), on the other hand, refers to a positive acknowledgement response that focuses on the child's efforts or specific attributes of work completed.' She goes on to argue that encouragement can focus on improvement and effort without evaluating an outcome, it avoids comparisons and creates an environment where mistakes can be made. This in turn develops resilience and an intrinsic desire to do well in the task for its own sake.

3. Regularity

There are occasions when rewarding needs to be immediate, however, it will also need to be gradual and regular. The needs of the child and the context in which the rewards are given will need to be taken into account otherwise we may fall into the trap of either under or over rewarding. Some children will need the immediacy of the reward sooner than others. For these children the encouragement gained from the reward will have limited or less impact if it is not delivered immediately or as close to the event as possible. However, there will be children who may not need each and every action immediately rewarded; in fact, it could be counterproductive as the rewards may become meaningless.

Encouragement in the form of recognition and reward at the end of a lesson, a day, a week (depending on what is being encouraged) could be sufficient. Deciding to reward immediately or gradually and regularly will reflect the growing ability of the child to engage in the appropriate behaviour because they intrinsically want to rather than behaving to the reward.

4. Relevance

A good reward system has to feel relevant for the child and the teachers who implement it. There are a few effective ways to achieve this. Firstly, make sure it is age appropriate. This is not as straightforward as it sounds and once again will depend on what encourages the child. The prospect of earning stars in Year 11 may not be as motivating as a voucher; what motivates one age group or individual may demotivate another. A good rule of thumb could be to look at rewards that involve encouraging appropriate behaviour by giving the child recognition, attention and time.

5. Value

A hard tangible reward scheme will only be relevant if it maintains the value of the currency. The coin in your pocket has a value only in the sense that you know what you get in exchange for it. The value will only be maintained if all pupils are rewarded and believe in the system.

Some children may need the added support of an individual behaviour plan. Individual plans do not mean different expectations, rules, rewards or consequences. A completely different behaviour plan from the rest of the school would be a form of exclusion not inclusion. An individual reward scheme as part of the individual plan should not de-value the main system of rewarding in the learning environment.

A pupil may need more regular tangible rewards to maintain motivation and reinforce appropriate behaviour. However, if they earn twice or three times as many house points than others in the learning environment for the same effort or perceived effort the value of the currency is devalued. The obvious unfairness may demotivate other children, disassociate them from a key pillar of the school behaviour plan, compromise school culture and alienate the individual from their peers. The worst-case scenario is that some 'turn up, do and go home' children will learn that to get a lot of tangible rewards it is better to operate within an individual system and behave accordingly.

The link between the individual and learning environment scheme of rewards should be explicit. An individual reward scheme may need to be more regular, often, obvious and tangible. But the scheme should reward more for the same effort, compliance or demonstration of the appropriate behaviour. For example, the unit of currency is broken into parts and the individual scheme reflects this. So, instead of earning a star each time a tangible reward is given, a point of the star is earned and 6 points equals 1 star. This will maintain trust in the system for other children as concepts such as fairness are not compromised. The value of the currency is maintained.

Real-life example

We were asked to consult and observe an Early Years' child who was struggling with challenging behaviours in school. He struggled to stay still during carpet time teaching. We introduced a differentiated reward system for him that fed into the whole class reward system, which was pompoms in a jar. (The younger the child, the more visual and visually present the reward has to be, they can only hold it in mind if it is visually present. If it is not visually reminding them, then it loses its effectiveness.) (Also, when you have worked in a special school, you refrain from using marbles as they cause damage when they are thrown.)

Every time, he was able to sit still (initially only for 10 seconds), he got a counter in his pot and when he had six counters, he added a pompom to the jar for the whole class. When he got his six counters, he was taken on a movement break. (We were always taught to end it on a good note, instead of extending it for too long and things failing.)

Gradually the amount of time he was required to sit still was increased and eventually he did not need the individual reward system as the behaviour was embedded. It was a joy watching little 4/5 year olds enjoy dancing with a disco ball for five minutes when they filled their pompom jar.

6. Simplicity

Make sure the reward scheme is clear and simple as this will assist in understanding and administration. Complicated schemes get in the way of managing behaviour and cause confusion. As with the rules, if the reward scheme is not clear and understandable children will not buy into it and teachers will not implement it. I have been in classrooms where some systems are incomprehensible. If you are in doubt about clarity, ask the children to explain it; if they are unable to, stop using it and think of something else. Do not be tempted to have lots of different systems going at one time. There may be some differentiation for individual children, but these will still need to link in with the whole school system to maintain a shared culture. A range of rewards separate from each other may lead to confusion and separate cultures in different parts of the school.

7. Implementation

It is also useful to think about how rewards are delivered or given. Does the implementation:

- achieve the aims of motivation and reinforce appropriate behaviour?
- get in the way of planned responses to inappropriate behaviour and the teaching of appropriate behaviours?
- merely contribute to a competitive culture?
- and the public display of rewards have the potential of causing anxiety, embarrassment or fear?

While competition may motivate some, the primary function of a reward scheme is to encourage and reinforce appropriate behaviour. It is not about children tracking their progress in relation to others, to reach the prize first, win the league by getting the most points and subsequently forget what it was they had to do to get that many points or how they got them.

A culture of competition, with public displays of the individual's number of stars or points, could be perceived as not so much about how well a child has done but how they are not doing well in comparison to others. It may focus the child on the system rather than reinforcing appropriate behaviour and not encourage intrinsic motivation to behave appropriately.

Reflection Point: Time to think about my practice

- Think about how it would be for you if your planning, your classroom observations, attendance, achievements or appraisals were displayed with others in the staffroom for all to see.

8. Keep it fair

Once earned rewards should not be taken away. This is because it keeps the appropriate behaviour the focus of attention. If an appropriate behaviour is demonstrated it needs recognising, encouraging and re-enforcing. There are systems whereby children can earn points for appropriate behaviour and have points taken away for inappropriate behaviour. The problem with this system is that it may seem unfair and unjust and lead to demotivation. It is also focussing attention on inappropriate behaviours. It may lead to a lack of belief in the process, over complicate the system and lead to misunderstanding as it is conflating two concepts: rewards and consequences. This will lead to confusion about both systems.

Reflection Point: Time to think about my practice

- How are my rewards displayed in the learning environment?
- Do I use a mix of rewarding that includes hard and soft tangibles, non-tangibles, verbal and non-verbal, short, medium and long term?
- Do I reward regularly? Do I keep the system simple? Is it fair?
- Is it easy to implement?
- Are rewards linked to behaviours? Do they understand why they are being rewarded?
- Do I maintain the value of the rewards?
- Are the rewards relevant?
- Do they reinforce appropriate behaviours, encourage and motivate?
- Do I reward those who 'turn up, do and go home'?
- Do I catch them being good?

Consequences

The third part of the behaviour are consequences. Probably the most important factor in considering consequences can be taken from Rogers (2011) who suggests their 'certainty is more important than their severity. Bennet describes consequences in his report 'Creating a culture as a conversation between the child and the school': 'The school culture's reply to the actions of the individual. That reply can either be to permit, to prohibit and discourage, or to encourage and praise. Without consequences, this conversation between the students' behaviour and the school's culture is lost. The simplest and often most misunderstood method of communicating the concept that actions have consequences.'

The way we implement this part of the plan is very important. Consequences can make for more problems or issues to deal with because of the way they are delivered. Unfortunately, sometimes consequences can be presented in a humiliating and shaming way. This could include making it public in front of their peers or making the consequence too severe. As the professional we need to ask ourselves if we are using the consequence to punish or change a behaviour.

A consequence needs to be given to the correct person. It is not appropriate to give a consequence to people who have not undertaken the inappropriate behaviour as this causes a sense of unfairness and conflict. Consideration needs to be given to how helpful whole class/group (blanket) consequences are as it may alienate the children who are behaving appropriately.

For example: As parents we were required to sign our sons' homework logbooks at the end of each week. One week we forgot to sign it (busy weekend – human irresponsibility), but this led to one of our sons receiving a detention as a consequence. We as parents should have received the detention as we were the ones who did the inappropriate behaviour. This led us to, in order to prevent him from receiving any more detentions for our behaviour, sign each week's log in advance for the remainder of the academic year as we could not guarantee that we would not forget again. This unfortunately did not achieve the intended appropriate behaviour of signing it every week.

While developing this part of the behaviour plan it is worth noting the different types of consequences. They usually break down into two categories: natural and logical consequences.

Natural Consequences

Natural consequences are consequences that happen without the direct involvement of the authority figure. In a school, this would involve allowing the behaviour of the child to continue to a logical conclusion without the intervention of the teachers. The theory being that by allowing the behaviour to continue eventually a natural consequence will occur that will prevent it being repeated and the child will learn the appropriate behaviour.

Examples of Natural Consequences

- Child argues about wearing their coat outside in the playground on a rainy day. They get wet and must come back in early.
- Child with underdeveloped play skills needs to control games in the playground. Friends stop playing with them until they have nobody to play with.

In each of these scenarios allowing the natural consequences to happen the child learns to change behaviour, wear their coat or interact with peers in a less controlling way. However, this is dependent on the child's cognitive development and their ability to link cause and effect.

A natural consequence may be more dynamic in the sense that if the child concludes on their own to change the behaviour, it is probably a more powerful learning experience. However, it is difficult to implement in the learning environment. Certain behaviours cannot be allowed to continue naturally and direct intervention by teachers will be needed.

The additional challenge with natural consequences is that they may not always happen immediately. Of course with the raining example, that is immediate, but with the child controlling the play, it may take several weeks before the consequence of the other children not wanting to play with them occurs. Then they may not be able to link the actions to the consequence.

Logical consequences

Logical consequences involve intervention by the teachers. Direct action to stop and change the behaviour. It is an action directly linked to the inappropriate behaviour. These are the consequences mostly associated with the school behaviour plan. Examples include:

- Child refuses to come back in from the playground into class after playtime. Has next break in class.
- Refusing to do work, receives a formal warning with continual gradual and graded responses if refusal continues e.g. written warning, time out, work with named teachers, detention, alternative arrangements at breaks etc.

Logical consequences are pre-planned and responsive not reactive. A reactive response may lead to interventions that are driven by our emotions. Reactions can seem personal as they tend to focus on the individual rather than the behaviour. This can lead to conflict and distract from implementing strategies and interventions to change the behaviour and teach the appropriate behaviour. The outcome is less effective as those implementing the consequence may overreact and could be perceived to be aggressive.

A proactive response is assertive and consistent; it is more effective because it is delivered calmly, other aspects of the behaviour plan can be referred to, rules and expectations are stated clearly, teachers know what to say, how to say it, when to say it. Because it is planned and prepared, it is an approach that is firm, fair and consistent. This approach is most effective when both teachers and child know what will happen next and is accompanied by a script that does not change.

Practical hints for creating effective consequences

1. Certainty rather than severity

The purpose of a consequence within the culture of a learning environment is to stop an inappropriate behaviour and encourage an appropriate behaviour. They do not work in isolation of the other key elements of the behaviour plan. They do not have to be severe to be effective. The principle of certainty is very important. Children need predictability and therefore they need to know that any consequence will be carried through and only when it is a certainty, will it begin to change situations. The severity of the consequence may have little impact at least less than the certainty.

2. Hierarchical

Consequences need to be hierarchical, gradual and graded. There needs to be a sequence that can deliver an appropriate response to low-, medium- and high-level behaviours. This will usually start with a verbal warning to stop the inappropriate behaviour. The verbal warning needs a script that is concise and clear. It will include an instruction to stop the inappropriate behaviour followed by an instruction to engage in the positive alternative behaviour. The warning allows the child to rectify the behaviour initially and begin to engage in the positive alternative behaviour. From this point there is a clear sequence of levels where the consequence gets more serious as it is implemented, going up a level depends on the behaviour. When implementing a consequence system, it is important it is well understood and clear to the child what each level will mean and the criteria for going up levels. This will support predictability in the delivery as will an accompanying script that is concise and focussed. There will need to be the option of a severe clause, where one can jump to the most severe consequence to immediately deal with the most serious behaviour that escalates quickly and is out of control.

3. Keep it simple

Consequences, like other aspects of the behaviour plan, need to be manageable. Keep it simple - if it is complicated, as with rewards, uncertainty will follow and they will be less effective.

4. Part of the culture

Consequences need to be seen as part of not only the school behaviour plan but the culture of the school. To achieve this, they need to more than just punitive. They will not be effective if all they do is punish. They need to stop the inappropriate behaviour and effect change whereby an appropriate behaviour can be learnt. They should be something the children do not like but they should not embarrass or humiliate. They need to be seen as fair. If they are perceived to be fair, they will be more easily accepted and therefore more effective. To achieve this, they need to be implemented consistently and with certainty in a calm and firm manner.

Reflection Point: Time to think about my practice

- How are my consequences displayed?
- Are they gradual and graded?
- Are they fair?
- Do they support the behaviour plan of the learning environment?
- Are they easily understood?
- Are they linked to behaviours?
- Do they discourage inappropriate behaviour?
- Are they linked to other parts of the behaviour plan?
- How do they reflect the culture?
- Is implementation consistent?
- Do I have a script that supports implementation?

Final thoughts

The behaviour plan in a learning environment needs a well embedded culture and ethos to support consistent implementation. The culture and ethos need a consistently implemented behaviour plan to become well embedded. One supports the other. It gives teachers ownership of behaviour in their classroom, the ability to plan for and teach behaviour and develop a culture where there are high expectations, clear rules and clear boundaries that are consistent and fair. The school behaviour plan is also a preventative tool in that it details a co-ordinated whole school approach to behaviour before issues arise. As long ago as 1989 the Elton Report stated, 'While some schools seem preoccupied with bad behaviour, others have made concerted policies for raising expectations and improving standards. The schools we saw which had such policies seemed to be very successful in creating an orderly and purposeful atmosphere. They marginalized bad behaviour by promoting good behaviour.'

The relationship between culture and behaviour plan is reciprocal. This relationship allows schools to develop a strong sense of community and promote opportunities to develop systems underpinning positive support for behaviour. It allows the school's core beliefs to promote good behaviour, it allows for practice that is consistent, it encourages teachers to model and teach appropriate behaviour routinely and reinforce it on a regular basis. Appropriate behaviour is genuinely recognised and rewarded, inappropriate behaviour dealt with fairly. It reduces uncertainty and promotes an appropriate climate for learning. Where an individual child experiences difficulty in developing or sustaining appropriate behaviour there are systems which give additional support. It is a relationship that includes all stakeholders and creates a learning environment that will flourish within the context of mutual respect.

Learning Points

- Rules are different to expectations.
- Rewards can be differentiated for individual children as long as there is a link to the class/school reward system.
- Remember the children who 'Turn up, Do and Go home'.
- Consequences require certainty not severity.

CHAPTER 5

Defining and Supporting Behaviour through the Behaviour Spectrum

> ***'True education must correspond to the surrounding circumstances or it is not healthy growth.'***
>
> Mahatma Gandhi

Ask any professional dealing with issues of behaviour in a school and, understandably, they seek practical solutions and look for the most appropriate strategies and interventions: the tools used to affect change, discourage inappropriate behaviour and reinforce appropriate conduct. While there is, and rightly so, a focus in schools on the type of strategy and the effect of that strategy, has there been enough focus on the process? In other words, why we do we choose one strategy or intervention over another? What is the process that a professional goes through to implement one set of strategies or an intervention over another?

The importance of relationships, the influences on behaviour, understanding what is behind the behaviour, and developing a clear culture and behaviour plan are all important concepts that should be key to developing our responses to behaviour. These have been dealt with in previous chapters. However, for the purposes of this chapter, we would like to focus on the process of how and why we choose a particular strategy or intervention, and to look at some practical tools that may help us choose the most effective strategy and interventions.

We would like to be clear that, for us, the starting point has to be acknowledging that there is no such thing as a 'bad strategy' or a 'better intervention', simply the most appropriate one at that time to meet an identified need. We are all very familiar with the analogy of tools in our toolbag when thinking about developing skills and knowledge. If we accept this analogy, we need to have as many tools in the bag as possible to make sure we have the most helpful tool for the specific task. If you want to change a plug a saw is not a very useful instrument; but we don't throw it away, we go through the process of choosing a more appropriate tool – the screwdriver. However, the saw may be the most appropriate tool for the task tomorrow.

Choosing the right strategy or intervention is similar. It might not work today but it might be the right tool for tomorrow, as the circumstances or context could be different, or the reasons why a particular strategy seemed appropriate could change. In essence, it is important to try to understand why the behaviour is happening before we implement an intervention or strategy. To help with developing our understanding and ultimately choosing the most appropriate approach, there are a number of things we can do to make the process more successful. However, before looking at the process of strategy selection, it is useful to explore the concept of 'managing behaviour'.

Behaviour Management or Behaviour Support?

While many different approaches and methods are available, solutions do seem to be presented within the context of the term 'behaviour management' and a common understanding of what that term means. Do all behaviours need to be managed? Is behaviour management (or our common understanding of the term 'behaviour management') the solution to all issues regarding behaviours of concern? Is it a term that is truly helpful or useful?

A simple search on the internet for a definition will say behaviour is 'the way in which one acts or conducts oneself, especially towards others' (Bell, 2013). Further reading of the definition suggests that there are expected standards by which we judge whether a behaviour is appropriate or inappropriate. A search for the term management will attract words like 'control' and 'responsibility'. The issue with the term behaviour management is that it implies the exercising of control over something in the here and now, but actually there is a stage before this that first needs to be examined – the stage of prevention.

In the school setting, when we hear the term behaviour management, we often assume there is an existing issue, concern or problem that has to be managed. If you ask a teacher to name some behaviours they have experienced, the vast majority of behaviours mentioned will be inappropriate ones (as discussed earlier). The concept of behaviour management assumes an intervention to change an inappropriate behaviour. The strategy or intervention come from a subjective assessment that something is broken and needs fixing. In other words, do we think of behaviour management as a way of managing positive or appropriate behaviours, or is it a tool used to fix a problem?

Imagine the classroom that is vibrant, creative and stimulating, in which learning is taking place and relationships between all in the environment are positive. Is this happening despite behaviour management or because of it? What if it is made possible because we are constantly and continually managing behaviour in our classrooms, not to fix something but to maintain and build what is already established? What if we are recognising the appropriate behaviours that are occurring regularly in our learning environments and using them as the starting point for our strategies and interventions?

Behaviour is constant in a learning environment; if we use the term 'behaviour management' it should be about reinforcing appropriate behaviour before being used to discourage inappropriate behaviour. Think of the phrase 'catch them being good'. Using tools, techniques, strategies and interventions that reinforce first and discourage second helps move the concept from 'behaviour management' to 'behaviour support'. If we accept that behaviour is constant and needs to be supported all the time, then the term behaviour support begins to make more sense and is more practical in terms of its application. It changes a process that starts with the perception that something needs changing to an approach that assumes something needs reinforcing and is only changed when needed. The implementation of strategies and interventions becomes a tool that meets the needs of all, not just a few. Behaviour support is not a discrete subject or a reaction to an issue, but a planned series of supportive responses and a golden thread that permeates everything we do in our learning environments.

Reflection Point: Time to think about my practice

- How do I catch pupils being good?
- Do I support and reinforce appropriate behaviour before I manage inappropriate behaviour?
- What strategies and interventions do I implement in my learning environment that are constantly in place for all?

Defining Behaviour

In Ireland there is a story told about a tourist travelling to Dublin who gets lost. On driving into a town, he stops and asks a local, "Do you know the way to Dublin?" The local replies, "I do but I wouldn't start from here". The story illustrates the importance of starting from the right place.

We often use woolly or unclear language to define behaviour, such as 'having a wobbly' or 'throwing a temper tantrum'. Every person who reads those statements will have their own understanding of what a wobbly or a temper tantrum is. Such terms do not objectively describe the behaviours. Defining the behaviour provides clarity for everyone who is involved or supporting the behaviour; it reduces confusion and enables us to find a positive alternative behaviour. In other words, it explains clearly what the child is doing and what you want them to do.

When defining a behaviour, it is initially useful to add '-ING' to the word used to describe it. For example, talking, whispering, shouting, working, walking, running, swearing, listening, writing, tapping, smiling, laughing, following instructions, asking, and so on. It is important that the -ING is applied to appropriate behaviours as well as inappropriate. This process of defining the behaviour will give the teacher a greater chance of accurately interpreting the behaviour and then using a more suitable strategy or intervention, thus increasing the likelihood of affecting change.

However, there is another very important reason for identifying both inappropriate actions and positive alternative behaviours. The precise definition of both will give us a clear point of reference for what we want to change and what behaviour we want to replace it. The inappropriate behaviour of tapping a pencil could be replaced with a positive alternative behaviour of using the pencil to write with, holding the pencil still or putting the pencil away. In essence, the most important factor in all this is not the behaviour management tool itself, but defining the positive alternative behaviour we want the child to engage in, depending on context and expectation. Real-life example: a child running down the corridor is told to stop running. The inappropriate behaviour is the running and, after being told to stop, the tool used is a script where the child is instructed to walk. The walking is not only the appropriate, expected behaviour but the positive alternative behaviour to running. The child may have had a context for running, unknown to the teacher, that made the behaviour reasonable for them. The child may feel, having been told to stop running, that hopping down the corridor would be acceptable. By defining the inappropriate behaviour, based on an accurate assessment of what the child is doing, the appropriate behaviour or alternative positive behaviour can be clarified and the strategy or intervention will have a greater chance of success.

With this explicit defining of the behaviour, the practitioner is essentially making a dynamic assessment of what the needs of the child are at that given moment in time. We therefore meet/identify/accept the needs of the child in that moment and develop planned responses, rather than assuming/perceiving what the identified need is and possibly developing reactive responses. The defining of the inappropriate behaviour and positive alternative behaviour creates the context by which the strategy and intervention can be implemented. This mitigates against the effect of a strategy being unsuccessful, as it not only identifies the need but also the desired outcome. The process of definition enables a response that can be specific, measurable, action-orientated, result-focused and tangible (SMART).

For every inappropriate behaviour there is a positive alternative behaviour. They are two sides of the same coin, with a clear connection between them. This connection is vital because it makes it explicit to the child what they need to stop doing and, more importantly, what they need to be doing instead. The strategy or intervention is merely the tool used to get from one to the other.

This approach is not very different from the assess, plan, do, review model in the SEND Code of Practice; 0-25 years (Department for Education and Department of Health, 2015). The Code states, 'The identification of SEN should be built into the overall approach to monitoring the progress and development of all pupils' (6.5) and goes on to stipulate:

'All schools should have a clear approach to identifying and responding to SEN. The benefits of early identification are widely recognised – identifying need at the earliest point and then making effective provision improves long-term outcomes for the child or young person. '(6.14)

Early identification is a process of 1) clearly defining the issue, naming (-ING) it or putting a definition on the primary behaviour (ASSESS), 2) defining the positive alternative behaviour or desired outcome (PLAN), 3) using this to inform the strategy or intervention (DO) and 4) recognition of positive alternative behaviour, if achieved or not (REVIEW). Review will mean some level of monitoring, evaluation and recording will need to take place, although, on a day-to-day or event-by-event basis, this process is informal and not officially recorded. However, the necessity to formally review may arise, in which case a more structured approached may be needed.

Reflection Point: Time to think about my practice

- What behaviours am I seeing in my learning environment?
- Am I defining them correctly?
- Do I know the positive alternative behaviour I want for each of these behaviours?

Interpretation of Behaviour

Once we have defined the behaviours, we can then interpret them. Our interpretation is vitally important in preventing us from reacting to the behaviour and helping us to develop responses. It is not an exact science and misinterpretation does occur, which may explain why some strategies or interventions feel like they do not work.

The delicate process of communication is something we take for granted and one that seems simple and uncomplicated. It is a process that occurs continually between teacher and pupil, and is probably the most important factor in the establishment of a good relationship and in creating an atmosphere conducive to appropriate behaviour. However, the complexity of the process needs to be taken into account. The Albert Mehrabian communication model 7–38–55 (1981) explains this in a practical way.

93% Non-verbal + 7% Verbal

Body Language	55%
Tone of Voice	38%
Verbal	7%

In essence, Mehrabian advanced the theory that communication is conveyed in three ways: words, tone of voice and body language. His model suggests that, while all three methods can be expressed at the same time, the paraverbal and non-verbal forms are of more importance than the verbal, and that body language is more important than tone of voice. The literal message, or verbal, accounts for only 7 per cent of the message, the use of voice, such as tone, intonation and volume, accounts for 38 per cent and body language accounts for 55 per cent. While all three elements support each other, the non-verbal methods are more dominant, and the verbal will only be convincing, or the message fully understood, if supported by the non-verbal. We almost instinctively believe and understand the verbal if it aligns with the non-verbal. If it does not, we are not convinced and can be excused. It's not that words are superfluous, but they need to be conveyed within the context of the entirety of the process. A clear script spoken assertively is a basic beginning for any teacher and a founding principle of any behaviour management technique. However, understanding or interpretation of the script will be affected by the way the words are spoken and what gestures or expressions are used to support them. If this is the case, the phrase 'behaviour is a form of communication' takes on a very important role in the learning environment. If behaviour is a form of communication, the behaviour of the communicator is open to interpretation by the receiver.

There are factors that may influence our interpretation and need to be considered. The message the behaviour is trying to communicate may not be overt and it may not have a verbal element. It may seem confusing at first: the non-verbal may be communicating one thing and the verbal another, the child using the behaviour may not be clear or not know what they are trying to communicate, and it may be based on an emotion that is not understood. There are also factors such as intensity, frequency and regularity that can influence the interpretation process. While all these elements present challenges, the teacher has the responsibility, and even a duty of care, to interpret that behaviour as best they can and choose the most appropriate strategy to meet need and affect change in behaviour.

Interpretation is a two-way process. While the teacher in the learning environment is continually reading the child's behaviour (the interpretation of behaviour also occurs for appropriate behaviour), the child is also interpreting the teacher's behaviour. It may be possible that a child makes a genuine mistake understanding what they have to do following an instruction from the teacher, based on the teacher's verbal and non-verbal forms of communication. The child may be engaged in an activity they genuinely feel is appropriate, but if they didn't interpret the teacher correctly this can come across as defiant or a refusal to comply. The teacher engages in a strategy based on their interpretation of defiance and begins to manage a situation that may not need to be managed. The child can become confused by this response from the teacher, as they are convinced they are being compliant. This misfire in the communication leads to conflict that is confusing and unnecessary for both.

However, this is part of a continual and dynamic process involved in the interaction between the teacher and the child. During this process, the relationship will grow, understanding of the child's needs will deepen and interpretation become more accurate. The following flow chart may be useful when looking at what this process entails.

Communication

↓

Behaviour

↓

Interpretation

↓

Response

↓

STRATEGY and INTERVENTION

The key element in this chart is the interpretation of the behaviour. When a teacher in a learning environment is experiencing or observing behaviour, they will act or respond to that behaviour. Even the strategy of planned or tactical ignoring is a decision to respond to a behaviour based on a given set of circumstances. The response to the behaviour is based on the interpretation of that behaviour – in other words, an inference about what the child is trying to communicate. The interpretation of the behaviour will dictate how the teacher responds to it, and this response is the strategy and intervention.

Strategies and interventions are in themselves not a solution; they are the tools used in a learning environment to change an inappropriate behaviour into an appropriate one. There are no wrong strategies and interventions, merely ones based on misinterpretation of the behaviour. Interpretation gives the teacher the ability to assess the circumstances in which the behaviour takes place and choose the most appropriate tool.

Planned Responses Not Emotional Reactions

(Rogers, 2011) states, 'while I have found many theorists very helpful in my practice as a teacher, and in my research as university lecturer and writer, my interest has always been focused on how to bring our 'philosophy', our values, our delineation of ourselves as teacher-leader within the practicalities and day-to-day stresses (and joys) of teaching." (p.6). However strategies and interventions are implemented, or in what context they are used, they are seen by many as the central part to any support plan or keystone to any recommendation. In the many years we have been visiting schools to work with teachers on issues of behaviour, it has been our experience that, while teachers may be interested in contextual discussions and in assessment of need, it is the 'What can I do to change it?' or 'How do I meet that need?' conversations that are viewed as more important. At this point, it becomes almost impossible not have the conversation about practical strategies and interventions.

It is perfectly understandable for teachers to want a discussion on practical interventions. Staff working with issues of behaviour not only seek but deserve this practical support, which can add tools to their toolbags. Concerns and issues that are adversely affecting the relationship between child and teacher deserve practical suggestions that can be implemented in the classroom. This is particularly important when the professional pressure on teachers has never been greater, and the added complication of a behaviour issue can make even the most experienced teachers feel defeated, deflated and deskilled.

In our work with teachers, we have never seen a bad strategy or intervention. We have seen a range of strategies and interventions not meeting a need and appearing ineffective. When frustrations and anxieties are rising, the strategies and interventions used by teachers are sometimes implemented in a reactive way rather than as a planned response. At that moment, it can feel that the strategy is not able to manage the behaviour or can even make it worse. The teachers may feel more deflated and defeated, the child possibly more isolated, and both may feed off their anxieties regarding the ongoing situation. Marie Delaney (2009) states, 'not enough attention is paid to our [staff] own emotions and how constant challenges can make us feel. The other side of the equation is trying to understand what is happening with these 'unteachable' children, to block their ability to learn' (p.2).

If the relationship has broken down, a culture of anxiety rather than safety may exist in the learning environment. The child and the teacher interact and operate in an environment of fear: fear of what will happen next, fear of confusion, fear of the lack of control and fear of each other. This can lead to a misunderstanding of the behaviour by the teacher – a misunderstanding of what is behind the behaviour.

As strategies and interventions are perceived to fail repeatedly, the belief that nothing will change can take hold. The 'I tried that and that, and they don't work' mentality takes over. Frustration and anxiety lead to reactive interventions, and strategies are implemented within the context of something having happened rather than trying to prevent it in the first place. In other words, responses are reactive not proactive. Relationships between the child and the teacher suffer, and the values and culture of the learning environment are compromised.

Kirke Olson (2014) looked at this issue, beginning with the fear of physical danger, citing how a shooting in 1999 at Columbine High School, Colorado USA changed a place of 'safety to a place of potential danger and real anxiety'. While this is an extreme example, we could also look to Maslow's model (1954), in which he contends that while physical safety or 'the most basic measures for feeling safe' are important, complete safety derives from both physical and emotional safety. Emotional safety is reliant on trust and is dependent on our interpersonal environment. A safe school creates a culture of physical and emotional safety.

We have experienced and observed this culture of fear in learning environments, where behaviour can become out of control, leaving all feeling both physically and emotionally unsafe. When this is the case, it is easy to react, possibly out of fear, rather than with a rational, planned response. While delivering training, a central theme is that all behaviour is a form of communication. The child engaged in a behaviour is communicating something to the learning environment. This could be something positive, such as 'I feel happy', 'I'm enjoying this activity, so I'm engaged with it', 'I feel confident, so I will contribute'; however, a child may also feel sad, angry, isolated, frustrated, tired, grumpy or unconfident, and will communicate that through their behaviours as well.

Reflection Point: Time to think about my practice

- When was the last time I reacted to a behaviour?
- What processes do I have in place to help me develop planned responses to behaviour?
- How do I make my learning environment physically safe and emotionally safe?
- Do I know what tools I have in my toolbag?
- Do I sometimes feel I have tried, that it won't work?
- Would I try the same strategy or intervention again at a later time?
- Do I interpret the behaviour?

The Behaviour Spectrum

Throughout this chapter, we have attempted to look at a variety of methods that mitigate against reaction and help develop responses to behaviours. The last piece of the jigsaw is possibly the most important and the piece that makes all the others fit together: the behaviour spectrum.

Viewing behaviour on a spectrum is an attempt to understand the cause of the behaviour and ask key questions.

- What is the purpose of the behaviour?
- Why is it happening?
- What is the behaviour communicating?
- What emotions is the child experiencing?
- Does the child feel emotionally safe? (The overall feeling of being not just physically safe, but emotionally safe as well, will affect levels of engagement: if a child feels confident in doing something, they will feel safe and will engage; however, the opposite is also true.)

These questions facilitate the development of successful responses, as the answers give meaning to the process of interpretation. For example, if the teacher answers the question 'Why is the behaviour happening?' with the interpretation that the child believes they can't do something, the response will be very different from an answer that concludes that the child is saying 'I won't do it'.

Behaviour can be represented on the spectrum by intensity, each section with its own colour code. We use the word 'intensity' rather than 'level', as we think it is more descriptive and appropriate. The term 'low-level behaviours' gives the impression of behaviours that are not serious, nor very disruptive, and easily managed. We have both observed and experienced the effect on pupils' learning in a classroom destroyed by so-called low-level behaviours.

The Components Sections of the Behaviour Spectrum

© Adobe Stock Photos

BLUE: These behaviours are the appropriate, almost unremarkable behaviours experienced every day by teachers from the vast majority of pupils in a learning environment. We say unremarkable because they are the expected behaviours, from the pupils we sometimes call the 'turn up, do and go homes'. These pupils need to be noticed and their behaviours reinforced. These are the pupils whose behaviour sets the agenda in the learning environment; these behaviours are our default position. These pupils feel emotionally safe, they want to engage, they are calm and relaxed, confident in their ability to take part, they will take risks or 'give it a go', they will look for support when necessary and accept correction.

The pre-frontal cortex of the brain is accessible. This is important as it controls cognitive skills such as problem solving, memory, language, judgement and the ability to appropriately communicate. The pupils whose behaviour aligns with the blue area of the behaviour spectrum are fully signed up to the behaviour contract and not only will they 'do', but they also intrinsically believe they 'can do'. Their behaviour may on a few occasions stray into the next component, but the response can be very low key. It can be supported with a short, scripted reminder, accompanied by the appropriate facial expression and body language. The key strategy for this part of the spectrum is to notice appropriate behaviours and 'catch them being good'.

GREEN: This is the first component involving inappropriate behaviours. These behaviours are by definition not serious – low intensity but not necessarily low in regularity. These pupils are not feeling as emotionally safe as those in the previous component. They may be feeling unsure, apprehensive or anxious. Their capacity to take a risk and give it a go is reduced; correction can be seen as a challenge, or as criticism of an already perceived inability to engage in the activity very well. The behaviours may include being grumpy, chatting, fiddling with equipment, rocking on a chair, lack of focus, lateness starting an activity or arriving late to class, not completing work, being withdrawn, not contributing, being distracted, distracting others and generally being disengaged. These pupils can sometimes appear confused, puzzled, not interested in the activity. Sometimes it is safer for these pupils to pretend to be disengaged, so that when they are instructed to re-engage, they can pretend they don't know what to do because they were not listening; even though this may mean a consequence, it is perceived as better than taking part in an activity they might not be able to do and risking letting everybody know they can't do it. Engaging is unsafe; opting out is safe. The drive for this behaviour is not 'I won't do it', but is based on the belief 'I can't do it'. It will also be important to be aware of the context and regularity of the behaviour, as the child may think 'I can't do it' for certain activities and 'I can do it' for others.

The response and strategies need to be delivered within the context of support and reassurance. We are saying, 'you can do it, but you need a bit of scaffolding and that's OK, we will help'. Using a range of strategies such as a specific script, providing hurdle help and time to process the instruction will all help. These will be discussed in greater depth later in this chapter.

- script – this is an individualised set of wording developed to meet the pupil's needs, and all staff use to de-escalate the challenging behaviour.
- hurdle help – this strategy is helping the pupil to overcome a hurdle that is preventing the pupil from proceeding with the task. An example would be for the teacher to write the first sentence and then the pupil continues with the next one.
- processing time – sometimes a pupil will need time to process the instruction and giving them time enables them to think through the task and begin.
- physical proximity – using our physical presence can be a non-humiliating strategy to gently cha\llenge inappropriate behaviours. Moving to stand near the pupil may be enough to moderate the behaviours.
- praising the effort – this strategy is about noticing, acknowledging and verbally praising the pupil's effort. For example, I can see that you have kept all the letters on the line.
- first port of call – some pupils will need the teacher to go directly to them first following class teaching to ensure that they have understood the learning and to help them begin the task.

- being kept in mind – for some pupils, they need to stay connected to the teacher and will undertake behaviours to keep the teacher connected; therefore, leaving them with a transistional object such as a piece of fabric that the teacher has personalised and telling them that they will be returning to them in a few minutes.
- developing independent learning skills such as the Brain, Buddy, Board, Boss technique, cue cards etc. Brain, Buddy, Board and Boss technique is encouraging pupils to firstly use their brain, then to ask a friend (buddy), then to look at the board and finally when they have tried the other options and still need help to ask the teacher (boss).

It's important to recognise that it is hard for the child, but with support they may begin to believe they can do it.

AMBER: This is the second component comprising inappropriate behaviours. These behaviours are more challenging, medium intensity, but not necessarily more regular than low intensity behaviours. The regularity of a behaviour can make it challenging; however, the intensity of these behaviours is what differentiates them as part of this component. The emotions associated with these behaviours are ones based in anxiety: the child feels more apprehensive, nervous, uneasy and concerned about what they have to do or have been instructed to do. The child is feeling emotionally unsafe – unsure of themselves, others and the learning environment. The capacity to make a rational decision is decreased as the access to the pre-frontal cortex is reduced. The behaviours now look defiant and are communicating not just 'I can't do it', but 'I won't do it'. This area of the spectrum can include all the behaviours listed in the previous component but at a higher intensity. The child is louder – shouting, laughing, singing, banging equipment and furniture – and just exhibiting general disruptive behaviour. Behaviours can also be physical and movement is now a factor. Behaviours can include standing up and wandering around the room, or going over to pupils in other parts of the classroom to disturb them. Refusal can also be confrontational, and language can be angry and offensive. While the behaviour in the green component will mostly disrupt the learning of the child engaged in the behaviour, these amber behaviours disrupt the learning of all. In many ways, the behaviour is a reaction to feeling emotionally unsafe and safety is represented by attempts to control the environment.

Strategies and interventions will include the previous responses of support and reassurance; however, the behaviour needs to be responded to (and, yes, probably managed) in a more formal way. The learning environment will need to have a clear behaviour plan, so while strategies are being implemented (see the section on blue behaviours), they will be supported by structure, boundaries, rules, rewards and consequences. These will be specifically referred to in the script and used to support the implementation of strategies. Make sure the child is clear about what is expected and teach the expected behaviour beforehand so you know they can do it. not just should do it. These pupils will benefit from knowing the start and end times of tasks. They should know how long they have to complete any piece of work, spend on an activity or to attempt any task or activity.

- Limit the time spent on a given task.
- Increase the level of adult support given to complete the task.
- Simplify the instructions.
- Focus the learning outcome on appropriate behaviour in terms of undertaking the task, rather than just the specifically curriculum-based learning outcome.

In this component of the spectrum, environmental restructuring may be useful. This can include seating plans, a specific workstation and carpet sample squares (these can be obtained from carpet shops). Strategies such as tactical ignoring (focus on the primary behaviour of concern), visual prompts (cue cards, voice level indicators, now/next boards, changes board), a toolbag of equipment, speech bubbles, fiddle toys (make sure this is accompanied by an 'abuse it then lose it' criterion), movement breaks, countdowns or count-ups can be used. The use of regular non-tangible rewards, such as smiles, nods and so on is important, as is verbal praise; this will need to be specific and praise the effort as much as the product. Establish a protocol for all the times when the child doesn't know what to do or finds asking for support difficult. This could include teaching the child how to use a safe space – a place they can go when feeling unsure, anxious or upset – which supports the teaching of self-regulation. However, ensure the child has ownership not control of the strategy: permission will need to be asked for and given to use a safe space; if it is used in any other way it can become counterproductive, as it teaches the child to avoid certain tasks or activities. However, appropriate use of a safe space gives the child a backup plan, therefore they may be less likely to become anxious, behave inappropriately or employ attention-seeking strategies.

Teachers may need to be very aware of offering specific support more regularly (this will need to be planned, time limited and reviewed) to specific pupils, using moving in/out techniques, specific script and processing time. Interventions such as meet and greet, lunchtime or breaktime arrangements may need to be introduced. The overall aim is to develop responses to a behaviour that is communicating 'I won't do it' but is still based in the belief that 'I can't do it'.

RED: The final component on the spectrum includes behaviours that would be the most challenging and serious. These behaviours are high intensity but may not be regular or frequent. The child feels no emotional safety and may engage in behaviours that make themselves and others unsafe. Anxiety changes to fear and the child is very unsure of what they need, is unaware of the needs of others and the environment can feel toxic. The purpose of the behaviour is based on 'I will do anything but what I have been instructed to do'. The child is unable to make any logical or rational decisions and access to the pre-frontal cortex is limited. Behaviours can be out of control, aggressive and violent. They include abusive language, screaming, shouting, running around or away, hitting, kicking, spitting, throwing objects, damaging property, and so on. Previous strategies used may have little or no effect, and the safety of the child and others is the paramount concern.

The approach here is to first contain and then bring a level of order to a situation that is out of control. This could include manipulation of the environment, instructing other pupils to leave the room, time out, withdrawal and the use of a safe space. However, a strategy will need to move on from this to de-escalate the behaviour and insulate the child from further distress. Here, previous strategies mentioned can be used, if implemented within a different context. This includes using a script where the child's feelings are recognised, communicating a clear limit about the behaviour and offering an alternative to support de-escalation. A specific plan of response needs to be developed, as these behaviours are most susceptible to reaction. The plan should outline very clearly how situations will be handled and contain information on the following:

1 the teachers who will be involved if an incident occurs

2 where the child will go in school to have time to calm down

3 if it will be necessary to contact parents

4 knowledge of any script that should be used to interact with the child

5 whether or not the child will return to the classroom setting or if they will be taught individually for a period of time

6 how supporting teachers will be summoned

7 how incidents will be dealt with after the event

8 strategies for prevention of difficulties in the future.

Part of the plan could also contain a section on physical intervention as a last resort. If it is decided to plan for this, the school will need a specific policy that provides a framework for planning and implementation, based on current government guidance. The plan will need to be written in accordance with this advice and appropriate training provided to all teachers.

The Behaviour Spectrum

A culture and ethos of core values and guiding principles needs to be established, which includes a behaviour plan for the learning environment and a behaviour-for-learning contract between all stakeholders. This is underpinned by relationships between adults and pupils in the learning environment.	
Emotions and feelings contributing to the behaviour	
BLUE	Calm, confident, relaxed, excited, happy, feeling both emotionally and physically safe, and connected with the learning environment
GREEN	Nervous, frustrated, anxious, apprehensive, uncertain and a little bit more emotionally unsafe
AMBER	Uneasy, tense, concerned, angry, scared, defiant, oppositional, unsafe and unsure of myself, my capabilities, others, the task and the environment
RED	Hostile, ashamed, fearful, enraged, aggressive, out of control, feeling very unsafe and unsure
What is the behaviour communicating?	
BLUE	I CAN DO IT AND I WILL TRY TO DO IT I am safe and engaged with and want to contribute to the learning environment. I have a capacity to take safe risks.
GREEN	A learnt belief that I CAN NOT DO IT I feel a little unsure and slightly disengaged from the learning environment. I feel a little emotionally unsafe, uncertain and unsure. I have nothing of value to contribute to the learning environment. My capacity for safe risk-taking is reduced. I need to avoid the task and/or situation.

AMBER	A protective action I WILL NOT DO IT I am feeling emotionally unsafe and very unsure of my role in the learning environment. I am disengaged, as this feels safer. I do not want to contribute or let others know I have nothing of value to offer. I have no capacity for risk-taking. I need to control the learning environment.
RED	A survival response I WILL DO ANYTHING BUT THAT I am very emotionally and physically unsafe. I have no capacity to engage. I want to get out of the situation. I have a complete lack of awareness of my own needs or the needs of others. I will completely disconnect from the learning environment in any way I can.
Responses to the behaviour based on	
BLUE	Acknowledgement, encouragement and reinforcement
GREEN	Acknowledgement, support and reassurance
AMBER	Continue with GREEN strategies and interventions with additional formal behaviour support approaches
RED	Continue with GREEN and AMBER strategies, interventions and formal behaviour support approaches with additional strategies and interventions designed to support, reassure and make physically and emotionally safe

Behaviours that may be experienced at different points of the spectrum (some behaviours will be the same but, due to differences in intensity, regularity and context, may be mentioned in all sections)	
BLUE	• On task, following instructions, completing activity, engaged and interested in the learning environment • Can work independently, asks for support when necessary, begins work promptly • Makes relevant contributions, seeks attention appropriately, takes appropriate care of work and equipment, accepts changes in routine • Accepts boundaries of the learning environment, aware of and adapts to the needs of others, make friendships and attachments, accepts praise, respects others and property, can share, accepts consequences, motivated by rewards (tangible and non-tangible).
GREEN	• Chatting, distracting others, daydreaming, making inappropriate noises, language can be inappropriate • fiddling, rocking on a chair • not having the right equipment, being late, lack of organisational skills • needs or wants attention on a regular basis, unable to independently begin or complete task, forgetful • ignores general verbal instruction, at times refuses support, finds it difficult to accept consequences • unable to accept criticism and/or praise, reluctant to make contribution to learning environment, voice level can be loud, avoiding behaviours such as going to the toilet etc., argumentative • friendships change a lot or don't last, lack of basic social skills, can't share or take turns, can seem OK one minute and not the next, can seem disengaged from the learning environment, lack of awareness of personal space.
AMBER	As with GREEN but with more intensity and regularity • Unpredictable emotional outbursts, shouts out, can overreact, can be disparaging about own strengths • needs immediate attention when sought, has to be first, can't share, can't lose • wanders, moves around or leaves learning environment without permission, absconding

AMBER	• distracts others regularly, has few friends, very critical of others, name-calling • needs to control activity, has to be right, can be compliant then defiant, triggers difficult to pick up on • destroys own work and equipment • can seem demotivated, lack of focus or attention, seeks verbal conflict as a way to avoid activity or situation • banging on tables, breaking equipment • excessive defiance.
RED	As with GREEN and AMBER but with more intensity and regularity • Aggressive and/or violent outbursts when perceived to be criticised, challenged or unfairly treated • Has few friends • Regularly leaves room, mid lesson, without permission • Screaming, throwing, hitting, kicking, punching, running, spitting.

Reflection Point

Alex was tapping her desk in the middle of the maths lesson.

Consider your initial response.

Now view it on the behaviour spectrum.

What would the responses to Alex tapping the pencil be for each colour? Could you do this for other behaviours?

BLUE	GREEN	AMBER	RED
Alex was tapping the desk as directed by the teacher in a counting rhythm.	Alex was tapping the desk as she had been sitting for a long period of time; her body was uncomfortable and she was doing it to relieve the discomfort.	Alex was tapping the desk increasingly loudly as she was worried about doing the maths, and she knew from previous occasions that she would get moved to work with the teaching assistant, who supports her to overcome her worry and complete the task.	Alex was terrified of failing at maths; she was standing up and tapping the desk very loudly and was threatening to throw the pen she was tapping with at the teacher.

The use of the behaviour spectrum as a tool gives a practical structure to the process of choosing the most appropriate strategy and intervention. It is intended to give the behaviour a context, provide a way of understanding the behaviour, of looking for the purpose to and meaning for the behaviour. If used with the other processes, such as interpretation and definition, it may assist us in developing responses that will lead to more effective support for challenging behaviour.

Throughout this chapter, we have explored the process of supporting challenging behaviour. This comes with an understanding that every behaviour is a form of communication and we, as the adults, need to define the behaviour, understand the context behind the behaviour, interpret it and then develop a response based on our interpretation.

Learning points

- It is necessary to define the behaviour as this provides a clear understanding of the behaviour to the pupil and to the staff.
- Every behaviour is a form of communication.
- It is important to understand the context behind the behaviour.
- Challenging behaviours are on a spectrum and it is necessary to understand where the behaviour is on the spectrum. Additionally, it is important to understand where our approach and different strategies are on a spectrum.
- Using the behaviour spectrum helps to provide a behaviour support plan for individual pupils.

CHAPTER 6

Different Types of Behaviour

> *'Fortunately, most human behaviour is learning observationally through modelling from others.'*
>
> Bandura (1977, p.22)

In this chapter, we will explore the types of behaviour experienced by teachers and demonstrated by pupils in the learning environment that need supporting.

With regards to behaviour, we can sometimes get caught up in the minutiae of every action, and then spend valuable time, resources and energy on trying to alter behaviours that it may not be possible to change or that don't, in fact, need changing. This is not to suggest that inappropriate behaviour should be condoned or accepted, but that the context in which it takes place needs to be understood. Therefore, it is important to have a clear understanding of which types of behaviours to focus our energies on when implementing strategies and interventions to achieve change. It does not mean we ignore or give tacit approval to some inappropriate behaviours. The main reason for trying to put the behaviour into context is to ask whether the child acted intentionally or with purpose. This will help determine if the behaviour is generated from a fear-based survival instinctive response or a cognitive thoughtful intent (see Chapter 3, Understanding Behaviour and its Influences, for further discussion).

Reflection Point

Robert was sitting at the lunch table and his drink ended up being spilt. Consider the type of behaviour.

Types of behaviour can generally be discussed according to five categories:

- human irresponsibility
- behaviour linked to child development
- learnt behaviour
- behaviour linked to emotions
- challenging authority.

Human Irresponsibility

- Susan is playing on the playground, and it is a non-grass day. However, her ball rolls onto the grass. She runs to get it.
- Peter, aged six, jumps into a puddle just before going into class.
- Rory goes into his bag at the beginning of science and finds that he has left his book on the dining-room table at home.

Human irresponsibilities are behaviours that we all exhibit and engage in. However, they are not done intentionally or with conscious thought. These are actions that include spilling drinks, tearing clothes, falling over, getting dirty, breaking or dropping things, and forgetting something. These are everyday, human occurrences. Originally, they were called childish irresponsibilities, but all humans do them, regardless of age. Take the example of a father telling off his child for accidentally spilling his orange juice; as he draws his arm back, he knocks his own coffee, spilling it everywhere. He did not spill the coffee on purpose, but he had been critical of this same behaviour in his own child. If the child had said, "I'm going to pour this orange juice over the table", was instructed to keep the juice in the glass but chose to pour it anyway, that would put a different hue on the behaviour. Whether the action was intentional or purposeful is vital in determining the response to it.

Within the context of our learning environments, pupils forget equipment such as pens or pencils, PE kits, planners; they chat in line, are late for a class, lose something they need, forget an instruction, break equipment, talk/laugh/giggle when they should not, and so on. Just like adults do, too. These behaviours are human irresponsibilities; they can be challenging but only if there is intention and regularity. Let us look at the example of forgetting equipment. The perception could be that the pupil was being disrespectful to the teacher and the subject because they had not arrived ready for the lesson. However, it could be thought of in terms of human irresponsibility. If the pupil does this regularly then it is worth our attention and time. But if it is one-off, is it worth spending energy on behaviour-managing the situation? If we provide the equipment on that one occasion, we immediately focus the attention on to the activity at hand and enable the pupil to access the learning. If it continues to happen, behaviour management may need to be considered. We may want to look at why it is happening and provide support, so the pupil will have the right equipment on each occasion.

How many of us attending a course have forgotten to bring a pen and notebook, or have left our diary at home on the table? It is not that we have intentionally thought we will not bring a pen, but we were probably thinking about how to get to the venue, getting the children to school, planning for the supply cover and many other things. It is now common practice when attending conferences or training to be provided with a pen and paper in preparation for the learning. This addresses human irresponsibility and enables the participants to access the learning. It is interesting that we provide pens for younger pupils and adults, but sometimes become critical of adolescents who forget their pens. On the topic of pupils not having, losing or forgetting equipment, the poem by Joshua T. Dickerson (2019) seems relevant:

I woke myself up,

Because we ain't got an alarm clock

Dug in the dirty clothes basket,

Cause ain't nobody washed my uniform

Brushed my hair and teeth in the dark,

Cause the lights ain't on

Even got my baby sister ready,

Cause Mama wasn't home.

Got us both to school on time,

To eat us a good breakfast.

Then when I get to class the teacher fussed at me,

Cause I ain't got a pencil

Although we tend to accommodate these human irresponsibility behaviours in adults, who have maturely developed brains, we are often intolerant of pupils with immature and developing brains doing the same behaviours. However, energy spent focusing on these behaviours is a waste, as we are unlikely to change them. Of course we want pupils and young people to develop organisational skills, but their brains are still developing and consideration needs to be given to this. We, along with their parents/carers, need to provide them with the skills to remember what is needed to access the learning. Visual timetables, to include equipment for both school and home, will enable pupils and young people to develop forward thinking skills.

On the other hand, if a child or young person repeatedly fails to bring the correct equipment for the day or subject, deeper exploration needs to be undertaken. It may be that home doesn't provide the child with the equipment they need for school. It could be that they do not feel able/competent in the subject, therefore they avoid bringing the equipment so they won't have to participate; this is particularly apparent in physical education (PE), as some pupils feel self-conscious of their bodies or their abilities.

The older the child becomes, the more self-conscious they become in front of others. Additionally, as they reach prepubescence and begin the process of becoming independent from their family, they develop a driving need to belong to others outside of the family. This becomes a significant influence on behaviour.

Real-life example

I (Sonia) used this type of avoidance myself when I was 10 years old. I had been asked to sew a nightdress; I hated the fabric and sewing was a new skill. I was worried about being laughed at by my friends, for not being able to sew and because of the fabric. I purposely chose not to take the fabric to school on sewing days. This went on for weeks and at no point was I asked why I did not bring the fabric. I just kept getting told off. Getting told off was easier than being humiliated in front of my friends. The nightdress never got made and the experience put me off dressmaking forever.

It is important to step into the pupil's shoes and see the situation from their perspective. A few years ago, we collaborated with a young person who had recently undergone some sudden changes in their home environment and had begun to display some extreme behaviours prior to PE lessons. Following initial management of the behaviour, we were able to ascertain the underlying reason for it: their own PE kit was at their birth family's home and they did not want to wear someone else's. After attempts to get the child's own kit were unsuccessful, the child was allowed to go to the school uniform department and chose a new PE kit. This alleviated their distress regarding PE lessons.

It is essential to explore whether the behaviours are human irresponsibilities or whether they are done intentionally. If so, deeper exploration needs to take place to identify the underlying need. From there, strategies and interventions can be identified and implemented.

Behaviour Linked to Child Development

Children and young people are on a developmental trajectory. They are constantly evolving and changing. Sometimes expectations are made of pupils that are physically, mentally, socially and emotionally beyond their developmental stages. There may also be additional reasons such as an SEN issue to consider. We often expect pupils to understand, remember, articulate and process information like an adult. However, pupils' bodies, brains, knowledge and understanding are still developing and require practice, repetition and more repetition to grow and mature.

Having a knowledge of the different developmental stages throughout childhood, and a clear understanding of brain development, is essential for managing behaviours. For example, generally, children cannot physically tie their shoelaces before the age of six. This is due to their cognitive ability and underdeveloped physical dexterity, making it difficult to understand the method and physically tie the laces. An awareness of this can prevent ineffective behaviour management strategies from being implemented, as the adult will recognise that they need to support the development of the skills necessary to tie shoelaces, rather than unfairly expecting the child to do it for themselves automatically.

Siegel (2010) describes the pre-frontal cortex (the thinking brain) as not being fully developed until a person's early twenties. This part of the brain allows us to think through our actions, regulate our emotions and emotional reactions, problem-solve, forward-think, plan and manage our behaviours. However, often adult-appropriate expectations are made of the child and their behaviours; for instance, you may hear an adult asking a child, "Why did you do that? Did you not think through what might happen?" It may be that the child's developmental stage had not allowed them to fully think though the consequences of their actions and behaviours.

This is just as apparent during secondary school years as the teenager's brain and body goes through a number of rapid changes. The teenage brain undergoes another growth spurt and, thereafter, a pruning stage (getting rid of any neural networks that are not being used regularly). It has even been noted that teenage brains fire up in different places to the fully mature adult brain. This means that, on occasions, the teenage brain may misread facial expressions and therefore react to the faulty information received (Morgan, 2013). Alongside this, their bodies go through physical changes and they grow rapidly. They often become clumsy and uncoordinated, as their brains need to catch up with the rapid bone and muscle growth; therefore, the pupil may regularly knock over their bag, trip up or spill things.

An area that is often mistaken for inappropriate behaviour is the underdevelopment of a pupil's play skills. The ability to play cooperatively with others is an essential requirement for entering school. However, sometimes the adults assume these skills are embedded, when in reality the pupil has not yet learnt them. A lack of skill level can be perceived as an inappropriate behaviour. Sometimes, we just need to teach the skills.

Real-life example

Louis was roaring around the early years class, emptying all the cupboards and then racing on. He had been doing this every day since he had started. Any time another pupil went near him, he roared at them. Other pupils were becoming scared of him and the staff were at their wits' end as to how to help him. Following a lengthy consultation, observation and assessment, it was concluded that his behaviours were due to lack of development in his play skills, which were three years delayed. His play actions were typical of a child of around the age of 12 months. It was agreed that he needed a key 1:1 adult; this person introduced a play development programme (Murray, 2014, unpublished) to develop his relationship and play skills. This helped progress his social, emotional and language skills, and enabled him to gradually ccess the learning.

Knowledge of pupils' physical, intellectual, linguistic, emotional and social development can support effective management of behaviour. Understanding what a child is capable of developmentally will support the adult in making appropriate requests and expectations of their behaviour and learning.

Learnt Behaviour

Humans learn by watching and experiencing; therefore, pupils can learn behaviours by observing others displaying behaviours. Most behaviours are learnt by watching and interacting with others. It begins shortly after birth. When a caring adult repeatedly smiles at a baby, the baby watches intensively and then begins to repeat the action of smiling. This is a learnt behaviour, and it develops the skills to initiate and respond in social interactions. However, this also works in not-so-appropriate ways, too. When a child frequently witnesses others using aggression or defiance, such as not following instructions, and the negative emotions associated with these behaviours, this can become the norm and may be internalised as the way to behave. This can occur within the home environment, the child's community and/or their educational setting. For example, a three-year-old child starting nursery observes and experiences other pupils hitting them and others, therefore they perceive this as how they should act and start repeating similar behaviours.

Additionally, pupils not only learn behaviours from watching others, but they are also being influenced by television, the internet, social media, films and console games. Children will recreate what they see and experience.

Learnt behaviour can be developed from someone or something inadvertently rewarding a behaviour. When we use the term 'rewarding the behaviour', we mean that the behaviour has met an underlying need, produced relief in some form, reduced the distress and enabled the pupil to feel safe. This may encourage them to repeat the behaviour, which then becomes learnt. Think of the cliche of the screaming child in the supermarket; they have been told they cannot have a sweet but are nevertheless given it when they make enough noise. The child's behaviour has been reinforced and will probably happen again. In a learning environment, a pupil may learn to engage in attention-needing behaviours, such as distracting others, talking out of turn, shouting out and wandering around the room, to draw the attention of the staff to them. If the pupil's need is met and the staff pay attention to them, the pupil's behaviours will have worked and they may undertake them again. The type of attention given is irrelevant: negative and positive attention is attention just the same – a negative response is better than no attention at all. To change this learnt behaviour, we need to initiate attention before the pupil feels the need to seek it.

Real-life example

Penny was in an English lesson, but her internalised belief was that she is unable to do English; to manage this belief, she needed adults' constant reassurance. It was noted that, in the previous year, she had started getting up and following the teacher around the classroom. She had begun distracting other pupils, engaging them in conversations, and always wanted to sharpen the pencils. When the teacher was unable to respond, she would shout and stomp out of the classroom. Each time she left the classroom, a member of staff would go to her and ascertain what was the matter. Penny then learnt that this met her underlying need for adult support during English.

Following a consultation and observation, we explored with the teacher how this underlying need could be met, without Penny needing to use these behaviours. Penny and the teacher worked together to help them both recognise when Penny was feeling unsure of her capabilities about English. Then a privately understood signal was agreed, between Penny and the teacher, about when Penny needed support.

In line with social learning theories and a behaviourist approach, behaviours can be encouraged by the consequences that transpired following the behaviour. For example, when a child or young person is anxious about writing, they may start talking, screwing up their work or throwing it around the classroom. One of the consequences could be that they are required to leave the classroom; other consequences include the reduction of fear, not being laughed at by others because they could not do the work, and not being required to do the writing in front of others. All these consequences may encourage the child to undertake these behaviours again.

Sometimes, adults can reinforce the inappropriate behaviour, either by responding to it and therefore rewarding it, or by not responding strongly enough to appropriate behaviours. When we do not respond to behaviours that we do want to occur, we may encourage the inappropriate behaviours. If we positively reinforce the behaviours we want, the pupils will generally not need to engage in inappropriate behaviours to gain attention. If we fail to pay attention to behaviours that are productive for learning, what encourages pupils to engage in and continue doing them? We all need positive reinforcement. A lack of noticing pupils 'being good' can cause issues that did not originally exist. This was apparent when a colleague introduced an individual reward system for a child whose behaviour was presenting a number of challenges. The child had begun to regulate his behaviours and achieved the reward. At this point another child, whose behaviour was productive for learning, asked, 'How naughty do you have to be to get a reward?' This does ask questions of how individual reward systems can be implemented in the learning environment without devaluing the currency or reward system used by all (see Chapter 7 for further discussion). Therefore, we need to ensure that we pay due attention to promoting, rewarding and encouraging positive behaviours, and not just assuming or expecting they will happen.

Behaviour Linked to Emotions

As explored in Chapter 3, many behaviours are initially fear driven. The child becomes overwhelmed by the fear and from feeling unsafe, so they undertake behaviours that will reduce the feeling of being overwhelmed and, in their mind, keep them safe. As pupils are in the process of developing emotional regulation, there are times when they become overwhelmed by their feelings and this can sometimes lead to them managing these emotions through their behaviours. Even adults with a more developed regulatory system will become overwhelmed at times and may react to their feelings or emotions rather than regulate their behaviour, such as by shouting at someone. Therefore, if we view these behaviours as ones that need regulatory support, because the child is struggling with big feelings, then we are more likely to respond from a regulated, nurturing and understanding state than from a judgement alone.

The sense of emotional overwhelm can come at any time, but often when our tolerance level is reduced. Our tolerance can be reduced by a whole range of factors, including tiredness, illness, hunger, pressure and fear. For younger pupils, emotional overwhelm can happen more frequently, as they are only just learning to regulate their feelings. It might come at times when they are feeling under pressure, such as performing in the school play, doing a spelling test, SATs or preparing for GCSEs. Their stress level is already raised, the bucket is full; it may only take the addition of one more thing and, before you know it, they are feeling overwhelmed.

Real-life example

Jinny, aged 15, was studying hard for her GCSEs and was on track to do well. The pressure was on when, suddenly, the maths teacher added an unexpected test for that Friday on things that Jinny did not feel she knew as well. She became so overwhelmed that she used self-harming behaviours to reduce the stress. Any other time, Jinny would have been able to tolerate the unpredictability, but because her stress level was raised, she had very little tolerance to cope with anything else. Unfortunately, the behaviours did reduce the overwhelm and, because Jinny felt better, she used them again for a brief period. The self-harming behaviours initially stemmed from a reaction to emotional overwhelm but then became learnt behaviours.

Experience of trauma and disruptions to attachment can also be reasons for behaviours linked to emotional overwhelm. Due to their life experiences, the child may not have fully developed their regulatory system. They may have developed behaviours to enable them to cope with the emotions arising from the trauma, their loss and their experiences. For example, one child we worked with had been involved in a house fire and, whenever he heard a fire alarm, he would freeze and then would try to escape, even if that meant he hit and kicked people to get out.

Behaviours linked to emotional overwhelm may be due to the human body's instinctive protective response to danger. There may be times when the child's behaviours may be a response to a real or perceived threat. The body will instinctively attempt to protect itself by responding in four different ways, known as the stress responses. (Cannon, 1915)

- Fight – aggressive defending
- Flight – withdrawal from the threat (run away)
- Freeze – become immobilised
- Flock/fawn – align and appease the threat (Walker, 2013)

Due to the instinctive responses, the pre-frontal cortex (the thinking brain) is temporarily shut off and the reptilian brain (survival brain) takes over. As the child's brain is developing, they will not have fully developed the skills to override these instinctive responses.

Real-life example

Paul was involved in a physical altercation with another child in the corridor when I intervened. As I responded he attempted to hit and kick me (fight stress response), but his eyes were glazed; it appeared he had little comprehension of who I was and did not have a full understanding of the situation. Then he raced away down the corridor, away from the threat (flight stress response). I followed him into the classroom he had run to and stood by the door. He was now at the far side of the room, with a table in his hands, ready to throw (fight stress response). He had not consciously engaged in these behaviours; his instinctive protective response had taken over and had done what it needed to do to keep him safe.

At this point, my role was to help Paul to regain a sense of safety and not to add to his stress, so that he was able to begin accessing his pre-frontal cortex. His sympathetic nerve had taken over (Porges, 2011). I stood near the door, noticed my own emotional state, and used a calm voice to say that I was there, he was now safe, and that the other child would not be coming into the room. I repeated this a couple of times, giving him physical and emotional space to settle.

Gradually, the table came down and he flopped, physically exhausted, into a chair. I could now gradually move nearer and offer support.

Flocking is a challenging behaviour to manage and requires early recognition and a team response to manage it. Thankfully, over our 30-year careers in this field, we have only seen it on a couple of occasions. It is when one or a few powerful pupils initiate behaviours and, because others feel scared by the powerful ones, they join in. It is safer to be aligned to the threat than it is to be on your own. The potential threat must, therefore, be lessened promptly. As with all behaviours, it is important to examine what the behaviour is trying to communicate and what the potential cause of the behaviour is.

Real-life example

At lunchtime in a special school with forty pupils, Toby, whose behaviours generated fear in many pupils, began to initiate others in challenging behaviours. They joined in (flocking response). Suddenly the atmosphere changed in the lunch hall and it felt terrifying. Toby was telling others to start throwing plates at the staff and to 'get' the staff. Our headteacher, who had experienced flocking before in his career, spotted this and then quickly directed the staff to address the needs of the other pupils in the hall. He and I engaged Toby and escorted him out of the lunch hall. By removing the perceived threat, the other staff were able to regulate all the others and, very quickly, calm was restored in the hall.

Challenging Authority

This is a type of behaviour that may need to be our focus in the classroom. This is behaviour that is obviously based on refusal to follow instructions and accept the boundaries of the learning environment. When challenging authority, the child either purposely refuses to do as requested or purposely does the opposite to what they have been asked to do. However, it is vital to check that the instruction or expectation has been communicated clearly and in line with the child's developmental stage. If these elements or criteria are in place, it can be assumed the lack of compliance is based on refusal and defiance. On the other hand, a perceived challenge to the practitioner's authority, in the form of an apparent refusal to comply with a request, may sometimes be the result of the child responding literally to the way the question is worded. A younger pupil, or one with needs related to development, may only just be learning to understand all the subtleties of the spoken language. In these instances, the child may be more likely to respond literally to the request, which may result in them answering "No" when asked to do something.

Real-life example

During an observation of a child who was reportedly refusing to follow school staff's instructions, the educator said to David, "Will you come and do your work?" David, who was playing in the sand tray, responded by shaking his head and saying "No." The educator said, "There, he is refusing." However, David was not challenging the practitioner's authority; he was answering the question literally.

To take any confusion out of the situation, the request must be based on a clear script. The use of scripted language will be discussed Chapter 8.

Challenging authority is a behaviour type that may still have elements of the other four discussed and this should also be considered. Behaviours that stem from challenging authority can be of low intensity (green), such as chatting, fiddling, distracting others, giggling or refusal, or medium intensity (amber), such as shouting out, defiance or walking out; they can also include high intensity behaviours (red), such as screaming, swearing, throwing objects or hitting. The child conducting themselves in this way may lack a belief that the teacher and staff are in control and that the boundaries are effective. The behaviours may be testing this belief and, if the behaviours are not addressed or managed in a firm but calm and consistent way, the child or young person may become more out of control as they begin to lack belief in the boundaries or the staff to implement these constraints.

With their actions, they are really challenging to see if we can keep them safe and contain their overwhelmed feelings. For pupils to feel secure and valued, they need us to set boundaries for them. If their behaviour is not addressed, the child begins to feel out of control, powerful (but this frightens them) and insecure. These challenges need to be managed in a firm, clear, consistent, calm and positive manner. Even with clear boundaries, pupils will continue to challenge; it is part of exploring the world and developing the skills needed for independence and adulthood.

Now let's look back at Robert's spilt drink:

Type of Behaviour	
Human irresponsibility	Robert moves his hand to get his knife and knocks his drink accidentally.
Behaviour linked to child development	Robert may only be three years old. His hand–eye co-ordination is still underdeveloped.
Learnt behaviour	The child sitting next to Robert spills his drink and others laugh at it. Robert wants the same acknowledgement, so he does the same behaviour.
Behaviour linked to emotions	A dinner tray is knocked over behind Robert and he jumps from a fear response. In jumping, he knocks his drink over. Or it could be that he has opened his lunch box and realised that he doesn't have the same as the other pupils. He feels embarrassed and ashamed, so he reacts by knocking his drink over.
Challenging authority	Robert has had a difficult morning in class. He lifts his drink up and states, "I am going to tip this over the table." A lunchtime supervisor tells him to put the drink and the glass back on to the table. Robert looks at them and says "No". He then spills his drink.

Conclusion

Behaviour needs to be viewed in context and with each individual child in mind. Some types of behaviour require more support than others. Some behaviours will happen because we are human and others will happen because we have learnt that they met a need at some point, even if it is not needed in the current situation.

Learning Points

- Behaviour needs to be understood within its context.
- There are different types of behaviour and some require more support than others.
- Understanding the type of behaviour helps to inform the teacher's response.

CHAPTER 7

Target-Setting for Behaviour

> *'It always seems impossible until it's done.'*
> Nelson Mandela

Why Set Targets for Behaviour?

It's fair to say that those who work in education, regardless of role or responsibilities, have probably had their fair share of target-setting and, if they are honest, may well be fed up with it. Words like 'evaluation', 'monitor', 'inputs', 'outcomes', 'key performance indicators' and 'milestone success criteria' are about as exciting as watching the deliberations of the Education Select Committee on the Parliament channel, and probably generate the same amount of enthusiasm. However, it is an area that needs to be addressed and the question of whether the process of developing targets actually adds value to the management of behaviour needs to be asked. In other words, why do we target-set, what do we target and how do we measure it? Do we target-set because it's a statutory requirement or possibly to record progress, success and outcomes? Perhaps it highlights areas of concern and informs staff, parents and pupils; maybe it helps future planning and development of provision?

The lack of enthusiasm for target-setting could be due to the fact that it looks and feels like a process that pays lip service to the real job of practical implementation and, at times, the actual plan or target-setting format used is disconnected from the real needs of the pupils. The targets themselves can look impressive, but how much do they really inform practice or contribute to interventions? They live in a folder or in a file until the formal six-week or half-termly review and, despite a little tweak, don't really change. The only valid reasons for target-setting are to change inappropriate behaviours to positive alternative behaviours, support the pupil in developing the skills to demonstrate these behaviours, assist the planning of and implementation of strategies and interventions, and enhance provision. Any other reason is arguably superfluous and irrelevant.

To avoid behaviour target-setting being formulaic, make sure the target is based on a defined behaviour, identified by an assessment process that establishes a need; this allows targets to inform the appropriate strategies, interventions and provision, and their implementation.

Assessment

When assessing behaviour, begin the process by asking why.

- Is it to clarify what behaviour causes the concern?
- Is it to obtain a baseline to measure how much the behaviour is happening, so we can track progress?
- Is it to begin to analyse the behaviour and gain some understanding for planning interventions?

Whatever the motivation, the primary purpose of assessment is to identify observable and specific behaviours that are perceived as problematic, with the emphasis on current patterns of behaviour. The information gathered will identify need and barriers to learning, and will help when planning intervention and appropriate provision. It will also provide a way of measuring progress. Part of the assessment process will include observation.

Observation

When observation is being used to assist in the target-setting process, similar questions to those asked about assessment need to be considered. The first question is 'Why observe?'

- Is it the systematic and accurate collection of visual evidence, leading to informed judgements and to necessary changes of practice?
- Is it to confirm what is already known or to determine factual elements such as when behaviours occur, the nature of those behaviours, possible triggers, what strategies and interventions are in place, what provision is in place and what is successful?
- Is it to analyse what we already know or think we know? The observation may highlight things staff were previously unaware of and, crucially, what others are doing in the learning environment. We may be observing to get a better understanding of the problem, to assess which interventions might help or to provide a baseline to review progress against targets.
- Do we observe simply what is happening and when, do we consider triggers, context, environment, frequency and duration? Does the observation process use time sampling, event or frequency recording, incident recording or is it a continuous observation?

SMART Behaviour Targets

Together, the observation and assessment provide the necessary information to develop the targets specifically and the plan in general. They will make the process more effective and ensure that targets are:

S Short

M Measurable

A Attainable

R Relevant/Realistic

T Timed

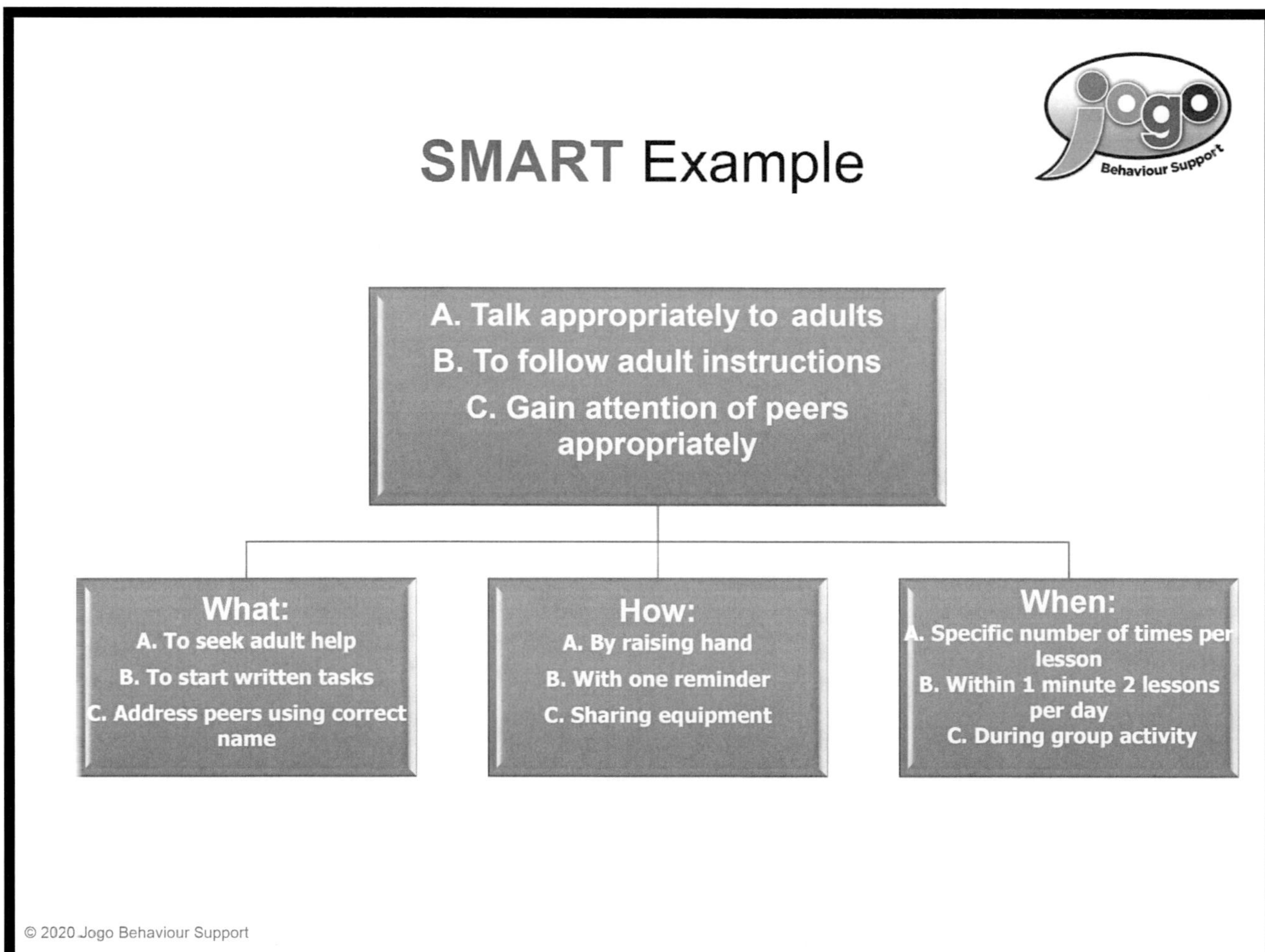

However we assess or observe, both should provide a definition of the behaviour or behaviours that are of concern. When this is done, the key to developing meaningful and relevant behaviour targets is making sure they include the following elements:

- The process can begin with the BEHAVIOUR EXPECTATION. This can be included in the target-setting process, but it is not the target. It is an overall aim or aspiration. It has to be developed into a target. The target is made up of three elements: What, How and When.
- WHAT is the desired behaviour expected of the pupil? It is important to remain specific about what the positive alternative behaviour is. What do we want the pupil to actually do? Each behaviour is developed on an individual basis. The pupil may have a target to put their hand up, but the teacher may also want this done with eye contact and without the pupil clicking fingers or calling out. These three behaviours would be separated into three WHATs on the target form. Decide which is the primary behaviour and work from that.
- HOW is the behaviour to be achieved? What support arrangements, conditions and resources need to be in place to give the pupil the best chance to exhibit that behaviour? This could also include several elements to support each of the three targets mentioned above. If the pupil has a target of putting their hand up, it could include a number of ways to support the pupil to achieve this; for example, a verbal prompt, a physical prompt, an adult beside them and a set number of reminders.
- WHEN has it been achieved? This is not just a narrow version of assessing if the success criteria have been met; it is also a description of where and when the behaviour should occur, or how many times or over how long a specific period of time. For the example of putting a hand up, this part of the target would include the context in which it takes place: at their desk, sitting on the floor, during group work, in assembly, lining up, in literacy or in some other subject, time or period.

This format will identify need and barriers to learning, help plan intervention and measure progress, establish success criteria and thresholds, provide small steps that are achievable, motivate pupils and staff, and provide clear evidential feedback that can be evaluated.

Considerations When Setting Targets for Behaviour

What is the reason for setting a target? As with assessment and observation, ask why a target should be set.

- Is it to change a behaviour?
- Is it to support a pupil to make that change?

- Is it to develop a positive relationship and create a stimulating learning environment?
- It is a requirement, to record progress, success and outcomes, and highlight areas of concern?
- Is it to support future planning and implementation of strategies, interventions and provision, and target resources?

Make sure the target does not lack clarity and is not confusing for the pupil. Has the inappropriate behaviour been defined and the positive alternative made explicit? Does the target have clarity? The target may reflect good intentions about the behaviour you would like the pupil to engage in, but does it have a clear purpose? It is difficult to accurately monitor and evaluate targets such as 'to get on with others in the class', 'listen to teachers', 'follow instructions', 'be kind to others', 'take part enthusiastically', 'try your best', 'complete work', 'show respect'. These are good intentions, at best general aims or expectations, but not targets. An effective target will contain information about what the desired appropriate behaviour is (the -ING), how it is to be achieved (How will they do it? What are the conditions and arrangements?) and, crucially, when the target will be active.

Some targets are not targets because they are not specific or measurable; they are statements about the issue or cause for concern. Examples of this are 'don't run in the corridor', 'don't swear', don't shout', 'don't wander in class', 'don't hit others', 'don't push in the line', 'don't leave the room', 'don't throw equipment', 'don't break property'. The problem with targets phrased in this way is that they do not allow success to be measured in terms of appropriate behaviour; instead, the focus remains on the behaviour of concern. For instance, if a pupil has a target of 'don't swear', feedback might be, "Well done, John. You swore at me four times yesterday, but only three times today." Or, if the pupil runs out of class, "Well done, John. You left the classroom five times yesterday and only four times today." The reason this is difficult is because the attempted target is a negative statement. It makes no reference to the appropriate or positive alternative behaviour and maintains a focus on the problem behaviour.

The purpose of the target is to clarify the desired and appropriate behaviour for both adult and child. If it is not specific or clarified it cannot be fully explained. The pupil may be unclear what is required of them and staff uncertain of what behaviour is expected.

Target-setting may put the pupil under pressure to succeed rather than support change from inappropriate to appropriate behaviour. If the target is expected to be achieved every minute of every day, failure is assured; if any of us were given a target every day at 09.00am and told to achieve it continually throughout the day, we couldn't do it, could we? Yet some target-setting asks this of our pupils. This only adds to the pressure they are feeling. It may also be appropriate to set the target within a certain context, such as at a particular time of the day or during a certain lesson, period or subject – if the assessment and observation support this. If, on the other hand, there is no evidence of concern within a particular context, why have this as a target?

It is important that the pupil sees the targets as part of a solution process rather than merely confirmation of a problem. The pupil may perceive the target-making process as simply being told what to do by staff, and this may compound a feeling of being acted upon rather than supported. This is particularly the case if the pupil has not been involved in developing the targets. The process of target-setting needs the involvement of many different stakeholders: these include professionals and parents/carers, but should also include the pupil.

How, where and why the target is presented needs to be given some thought. If an individual's target is overtly displayed, it may make the pupil feel singled out or even picked on. The displayed target advertises to the whole learning environment that John has an issue; this may make him feel apart from others, isolated and different. If the target is presented or written by 'don'ts', rather than the positive alternative behaviours or 'dos', the pupil will know what not to do but will not know what to do. The process is only partially successful as targets based on 'don't' may stop the inappropriate behaviour but not support the pupil to do the positive alternative behaviour. They may feel they need to be scripted to act up these behaviours and behave to the target.

Be careful about the use of rewards to support target-setting. An individual reward scheme that only John can earn, and only then if he is on target, may put pressure on him or compound the feeling of isolation, as it reinforces his separateness.

If these pitfalls are avoided, then the process of target-setting for behaviour will become more relevant. The inappropriate behaviour is identified, the destination to success is clear, the support the pupil needs to succeed is clear and the context in which the positive alternative behaviour takes place is explicit.

Format for Setting Targets: Examples

Behaviour Expectation	WHAT (Observable behaviour)	HOW (Conditions or arrangements for support)	WHEN (Success criteria, time, event)
Enter and leave rooms appropriately, without distracting others.	1 Walk from the playground to the classroom, holding a bag/equipment with both hands.	a) Walking with another adult	
		(b) On their own with an adult observing	
		(c) Alongside another child	Twice a day
	2 Walk from the playground to the classroom, holding a bag/equipment in one hand, with the other hand down by their side.	(a) With an adult walking alongside them	On each occasion
		(b) On his/her without own adult supervision	4 times a week
		(c) Holding a peer's hand with only one prompt	Lunchtimes
	3 Walk from the playground to the classroom, while using a quiet voice and kind hands. (encourage children to use gentle, non-violent actions with their hands instead of hitting or hurting others).	(a) With an adult walking alongside them	Breaktimes
		(b) On their own, with an adult observing	After PE
		(c) Alongside another child and with no prompt or supervision	
Enter any classroom setting using an appropriate voice level, wearing the correct uniform and having all equipment to meet the behaviour-for-learning ethos.	1 Enter each room without making a comment/saying hello/greeting staff. A teacher will be waiting at the door to meet and greet.	(a) Teacher waiting at the door to meet and greet	
		(b) Walking in and communicating using a prepared script/with appropriate voice level	For at least 3 out of 5 lessons
		(c) Walking in without any adult assistance	
	2 Enter classroom, communicating appropriately and wearing full uniform.	(a) With an adult at the door to give a reminder	
		(b) On their own, with an adult observing throughout	90% of lessons attended
		(c) Without any greeting or prompt	
	3 Enter a room, communicating appropriately and in full uniform, and have equipment for learning.	(a) With an adult to greet and give the appropriate reminders	Every lesson attended
		(b) On their own, with an adult observing	
		(c) Unaided in any way, without reminder or prompt	

In both examples, the format is presented in a very structured way, although it does lend itself to simplification and flexibility. The box with the observable behaviours can become increasingly complex, depending on the conditions in which the behaviour occurs. The use of simple annotation or colour coding to record when positive alternative behaviours have been observed helps provide evidence towards the achievement of the target. At any point in its development, only one element has to change to make it a new target. These examples are about individual[ised] targets; therefore, the same format cannot be used for a group or cohort.

This examination of target-setting began by looking at the elements that make behaviour targets relevant and practical. The format suggested is designed to give staff a workable tool to enhance practice, focus on specific need and improve decision-making about the best strategy, intervention or technique for each individual situation. However, the core motivation will always be to work with the child or young person in changing a behaviour and, with small achievable steps, provide them with the capacity and desire to do so.

Developing Behaviour Targets

Behaviour Expectation	WHAT (Observable behaviour)	HOW (Conditions or arrangements for support)	WHEN (Success criteria, time, event)
Talk appropriately to adults	Respond to questions	In full sentences	Every lesson
	Seek adult help	In words	___ lessons per week
	Participate in a conversation	In pictures	Specific lesson
	Use appropriate/kind words	Politely	___ tasks per day/week
	Contribute during group discussion	Verbally	Specific activity/task
	Answer questions when asked directly	In a quiet voice	____ number of times day/ lesson/week
	Answer indirect questions	In a table/partner voice	For ___ minutes
	Answer name when called	Making eye contact	In ____ minutes
	Answer at least one question	By raising hand	Assemblies
	Raise hand before speaking	By waiting for a turn:	Lunchtimes
	Wait turn to speak	• in a group of 2	Breaktimes
Talk appropriately to peers	Give task-specific comment	• in a group of 3	When asked
	Use appropriate voice level	• in a group of 4	On each occasion
	Make positive comments	• At lunchtime	
	Ask for equipment from peers	• At breaktime	
	Get peer attention appropriately	• In unstructured situations	
	Listen to others	Without demonstrating aggression	
Show respect to others	Respond to questions	During whole/small class discussion	
	Use appropriate voice levels	During lunchtime	
	Join in group work	Without swearing	
	Express an opinion	Within □ minutes of instructions given	
	Articulate needs appropriately	With 1 adult reminder	
Follow instructions	Share equipment	With a partner	
	Wait your turn	With all equipment to hand	
	Ask before borrowing something	By looking at the person speaking	
	Show awareness of personal space	Sitting still	
	Avoid pushing in line	Without fidgeting	

<table>
<tr><th>Behaviour Expectation</th><th>WHAT
(Observable behaviour)</th><th>HOW
(Conditions or arrangements for support)</th><th>WHEN
(Success criteria, time, event)</th></tr>
<tr><td>Show respect to others</td><td rowspan="3">Attend lesson
Stay in seat
Sit next to adult
Use kind hands, feet and words
Start a written task
Start a practical task
Listen to staff
Look at staff
Act on an instruction
Sit on the carpet
Work independently
Work with a partner
Work as part of a group
Complete specific task
Accept adult help
Have necessary equipment
Work/play alongside others
Work/play directly with others
Take turns
Use acceptable forms of physical contact
Take part in an activity
Describe feelings
Accept changes in routine</td><td rowspan="3">Keeping hands and feet to themselves
Sharing equipment
By writing a specified amount
Writing sentences
The first time of being given the instruction
By returning on first request
Maintaining suitable distance between self and others
Walking appropriately/slowly/safely
When following class routines
At the start/end of lesson
Specific lesson
Lining up/clearing away/getting equipment
In response to name
In new situations
Using a quiet voice
Without shouting
Without aggression
Without swearing
Without adult reminders
With another pupil
In unstructured situations
During change of activity
In assemblies
In routine class/subject activities</td><td rowspan="3"></td></tr>
<tr><td>Follow instructions</td></tr>
<tr><td>Interact appropriately with others</td></tr>
</table>

Learning points

- Target setting should be a tool to support the development of positive behaviour.
- Targets need to be smart.
- Make sure the target tells the pupil what to do rather than what not to do.
- Make sure the target is specific about when the pupil needs to engage in the positive behaviour.
- Ensure the target outlines the support the pupil will need to achieve the desired outcome.

CHAPTER 8

Strategies and Interventions

> *'If the only tool you have is a hammer, it is tempting to treat everything as if it were a nail'*
>
> Abraham Maslow 1966

There are a whole host of strategies and interventions that can be used to manage behaviour. Some of them may be effective for whole-school, whole-class or small-group situations, while others may be more useful for supporting an individual pupil. Before any strategy or intervention can be implemented, a clear understanding of the underlying need or cause of the behaviour is required.

Behaviour support strategies exist on three levels: whole school, year group/classroom and individual. By definition, the whole-school strategy will define the approach and direction the school will take to implement its behaviour policy, linked to its values and culture. Year group and individual strategies outline the organisational and practical ways this is done. A robust and successful strategy will have clearly defined links with all levels.

The word 'strategy' can be multifaceted in a school setting. A whole-school strategy refers to the overall strategy of the school. It determines how the school, as a whole, supports and enhances behaviour. Whole-class strategies are concerned with the classroom strategies in each individual lesson but are also linked with the whole-school objectives. While individual child strategies are implemented specifically for an individual, they must also link to the whole-class and whole-school strategies.

An intervention can be defined as an action taken to intentionally become involved in a situation in order to improve it or prevent it from getting worse (Cambridge University Press, 2022d). An intervention can be actioned following the identification of an area of need. Therefore, an intervention can exist on all three levels.

There are many strategies and interventions to choose from and a whole of host of people have written about them. Everyone brings their own viewpoint. In this section, we will be exploring different strategies and interventions that we have found useful over the years. Every child and every situation is different, and we need to carry the biggest strategies-and-interventions toolbag we can manage to support the complexity of needs found in a school.

Although we have been delivering training on behaviour support for over 30 years now, we still attend behaviour support training for ourselves each year, as we need to refresh and challenge our thinking and jiggle up our behaviour strategies toolbag (some tools will have dropped to the bottom of the bag and become buried under others).

One of the most effective ways of identifying the underlying need or cause is observing the child for a period of time. Correspondingly, gathering the child's history – including previous experiences in other classes or schools – provides a holistic view of the child. Time constraints often impact on this, so only some of the information is gathered. However, the most important aspect is knowing ourselves and our responses, as well as the pupils in front of us, understanding the context and assessing the situation, as this will help us decide on the most appropriate strategy or intervention at the time. Sometimes, we may have to react in the moment; but, afterwards, a clear strategy and interventions will need to be identified and implemented, in case that situation arises again.

Positive Instructions

Positive instructions are a necessity for behaviour support. Children do not have the cognitive maturity of adults; their bodies and brains are still developing. Therefore, when communicating with children, clarity is essential. It stops confusion, frustration and misunderstanding. Children need simple, clear instructions to ensure that they know exactly what to do and what is expected of them at all times. Adults often use negative or unclear statements such as:

- Don't run!
- What are you supposed to be doing now?
- Tell me what you should be doing.
- Why are you not doing what you are supposed to be doing?

None of these statements communicate what the child should actually be doing.

> **Reflection Point**
>
> List statements that you hear in schools, which may be unclear or fail to communicate what the child is expected to do.

Let us focus on the use of 'don't'. 'Don't' is a word that is used frequently in schools, but it does not communicate what the child is required to do. Young pupils, pupils with special educational and medical needs, and pupils with English as an additional language will generally only hear the last few words of a sentence and, therefore, will only hear the action that we do not want them to do. Some pupils, due to their underdeveloped cognition, may not process the entire statement and will, therefore, do the undesired action.

> **Reflection Point**
>
> 'Don't think about a red balloon.'
>
> Read this statement and think about what is automatically in your thoughts.

Most people when asked this, will say that they are thinking about a red balloon. Therefore, when we say 'don't run' to a child, we are planting 'run' into their brains and not actually telling them what they need to do. The actual action that the adult wants is for the child to walk, but this has not been communicated.

When we use the word 'don't', the child has to go through five cognitive processes to undertake the action.

Adult says 'don't run'	
Cognitive process 1	'Run' is planted in the child's brain.
Cognitive process 2	The child needs to remove 'run' from their brain because that is not what the child is required to do.
Cognitive process 3	The child needs to guess what the adult wants them to do. The adult has not communicated what the child needs to do. For example: • skip • hop • jump • twirl • walk?
Cognitive process 4	The child needs to choose an action and hope it is the right one, e.g. walk.
Cognitive process 5	The child needs to process the choice and do the action, e.g. walk.

If, instead, we use the statement 'you need to' with the clear action at the end, the child only needs to use two cognitive processes.

Adult says 'you need to walk'	
Cognitive process 1	The desired action – 'walk' – is planted in the child's brain.
Cognitive process 2	The desired action – 'walk' – is processed, and the child does the action, i.e. walks.

When we started introducing the terminology 'you need to' into our school's language in 2000, it was hard to implement as 'don't' had been our 'go to' vocabulary. It was like learning a new language; it took time, practice and lots of mistakes. Eventually, though, it became embedded in our everyday language.

Reflection Point

Consider some of the 'don'ts' that are used in schools and write the 'you need to' alternative. This helps to embed the 'you need to' statements in your brain.

'Don't' statement	Alternative 'you need to' statement
Don't run	You need to walk
Don't shout	You need to use a quiet voice

Questions should not be used when giving a behavioural instruction. Questions indicate there is a choice. Sometimes, if there is a clear choice, then of course a question can be asked. However, when we phrase a behaviour instruction as a question – such as, "Can you start your work now?" – the child might answer the question literally, with a "Yes" or "No" answer. This may be due to their age, cognitive understanding and any learning and/or medical needs. Examples of questions that may lead to a "Yes" or "No" answer are:

- Can you … ?
- Will you … ?
- Would you like to … ?
- Please could you … ?

We need to give the instruction as a clear statement, to remove ambiguity about whether or not the action is a choice. If the adult phrases the instruction as a question, the child should not be blamed for responding "No"; the adult needs to view the child's response as a literal answer, and not interpret it as a deliberate challenge to their authority.

Instructions should always be backed up with praise as the child begins to comply. Instructions will not be continually repeated and, if a child continues to ignore a specific instruction, a supporting and/or different strategy may be used. Always follow the rule of telling a child to do something three times, with reminders of expectations being given before the first consequence level is issued. This ensures a consistent approach to managing behaviour.

Another important point about positive instructions is to do with limit-setting. Landreth (2012) provides a model of positive language for limit-setting called ACT, which aims to reduce the areas of conflict. Landreth states that it is important 'to act rather than react in response to behaviours' (2012, p.273). We find this model useful, as it acknowledges the child's feelings (therefore developing their emotional understanding and helping them feel heard and understood), provides a clear instruction and offers an alternative so that the child feels they have an element of control. There are three elements to this approach:

A = Acknowledge the child's feelings, wishes and wants

C = Communicate the limit

T = Target acceptable alternatives

Real-life example: Sinead is swinging on her chair and is not undertaking the written activity:

A = I can see that it is hard to get started today.

C = You need to put all four feet of the chair on the floor.

T = I can write the short date, while you think of your first sentence. Or, to get started, you could move to work with Julie.

William is destroying his work:

A = I can see that you are cross/upset with your work.

C = You need to put your work on the table.

T = You can have two minutes sitting in the book corner or you can doodle on a piece of paper before trying again.

For some pupils who are exhibiting behaviours that lack internal controls and are impulse driven, teachers may need to use I-ACT (Cerio, 2000). This involves interrupting (I) the behaviour by clearly stating either the child's name or 'stop' before using the ACT approach.

When it is necessary to give a reminder of expectations or a direct consequence, avoid using terms of endearment such as 'darling' or 'sweetheart', as this can lead to confusion on the child's part. It is also unnecessary to use terms such as 'please' and 'thank you', as both terms can lead to further confusion and could, in some cases, be seen as pleading, condescending or sarcastic terms.

Teaching before Monitoring

Before 'managing' any behaviour, it is necessary to ensure the expected behaviour has been taught, learnt and understood in the first place. Children who are receiving good enough care from birth are being taught how to behave by their parents/carers continuously. For example, they are being taught how to:

- behave when eating
- behave with others
- behave when they are frustrated
- use please and thank you
- behave in the cinema
- behave when crossing the road
- behave when at school.

All behaviour is underpinned by our lived experiences, skills and knowledge. Not all pupils in schools have the same skills, knowledge and abilities. What we do know is that behaviour can be taught and improvements can be made. We can teach the behaviour necessary for school. A few examples are how to behave:

- when lining up
- when entering a classroom
- to be ready for learning
- when using school equipment
- when asking for help
- when answering a question
- when sitting on the carpet for the teaching input
- when a cover teacher is taking the class.

Lessons such as PE and science may have fewer behaviour challenges, as the pupils are repeatedly taught how to behave around the equipment. We find it interesting that the further up the school the child goes, the less the behaviour expectations are taught. If you go into any early years setting, you will see the teachers starting each day by educating the pupils how to behave.

It is important to remember that lots of school behaviours differ from what pupils are required to do in their home setting, so they sometimes forget what to do. There may be similarities, but there are also some differences. Schools only have pupils for 13 per cent of a full calendar year, the remaining 87 per cent is influenced by others, and by things such as media, outside of school. With this in mind, we need to keep teaching behaviour to pupils in school, whatever their age. In secondary schools, each subject teacher will have their own expectations about behaviour in their lessons, but they may only see those pupils for one hour a fortnight. In the meantime, pupils may have been taught by 15 other teachers, each with their own behaviour expectations.

Reflection Point

Remember to teach/remind your pupils the behaviour expectations every session – do not assume they already know or have remembered.

Records may be kept (that is, monitoring) as to how many times a behaviour has occurred, where and when. Observations can also be useful to provide the context in which the behaviour occurs and determine how the child is interacting with the learning environment. However, recording and observations are not interventions, as they only tell what happens, not how to respond to it.

The behaviour plan (discussed in chapter 4) provides a useful framework for establishing consistently the appropriate behaviour within the learning environment, and can be a reference point for subsequent strategies and interventions. In the context of teaching behaviour, we will need to make reference to rules and expectations that need to be followed. It must also be clear that appropriate behaviour is rewarded, while inappropriate behaviour has a consequence.

Environmental Restructuring

Environmentally restructuring is not just about where an individual child is seated; it is about the whole environment of the classroom. Sometimes just changing the layout, removing some furniture, addressing the sights, sounds and smells can change behaviour.

Real-life example

We were invited to observe a Year 5 class who were presenting the teacher with a range of challenging behaviours. The teacher had inherited the classroom after the Christmas break. On arrival, I noticed the smell; it was a small classroom, containing prepubescent pupils. It did not smell inviting. It felt hot and stuffy. The tables were set in groups, pupils had their backs to the board and, due to the size of the room, little space was left to move around; children had to step over the backs of chairs to get equipment. Their personal space was being stepped into regularly. (Remember what it feels like when someone stands too close to you in a queue? They have stepped into your personal space.) The room was jammed with storage furniture, there were displays hanging low from the ceiling, constantly moving and making flapping sounds. The classroom felt cluttered, busy and enclosed.

At the end of the observation, I asked the teacher how she felt teaching in this classroom. She stated that she disliked it. She felt enclosed and was constantly worried about knocking pupils as she moved around the room. She also felt disconnected from certain pupils because she could not comfortably reach them. If this is how the teacher experienced it, then it is safe to say that the pupils had a similar feeling.

We discussed environmentally restructuring the classroom. Due to the size of the room, group tables did not work, so the teaching staff settled on rows. This allowed the teacher and pupils to move freely, without stepping into each other's personal space. The teaching staff came in through the Easter break and cleared the excess storage. Additionally, we discussed how to reduce some of the sensory aspects of the classroom.

I arranged to visit three weeks after the Easter break. I was greeted by the teacher, who had a big smile on her face. She informed me that the behaviour issues had decreased significantly, but, most importantly, she said she liked being in her classroom now. What a difference.

Reflection Point

Take a few moments to stop, look, listen and smell your learning environment.

- What does it feel like to you?
- How might it look and feel to the pupils? If they are little, squat down and see it from their eyeline.

Consideration Point

One size does not fit all.

In primary schools, you can assess your class and your classroom in the first term or so. Do not assume that group tables will work with your current class because it worked with your previous one. Every cohort will need the learning environment to be restructured to meet their needs and the class dynamics. It is more challenging for secondary schools as the classroom needs to cater for a range of cohorts, and there is often not time to adjust the space before each lesson. This is where a seating plan can be helpful. This could be a written seating plan for the tables or desks, but it can also be for carpet-time teaching. Consider pupils' personal space when they are sitting on the carpet. Using masking tape or a sectioned rug can help delineate each child's space.

Reflection Point: Time to think about my practice

In a special school we worked in, the pupils needed larger personal spaces and were often unable to maintain their designated space without a visual reminder. We went to the local carpet retailer and asked them for squares from their carpet sample books. These were the perfect size for an identified seating space. Also, because they had a clear edge, it helped to visually define the space.

Think about your classroom. What seating plans do your class need? How can you facilitate this?

Seating arrangements in classrooms can be crucial in influencing how individuals may behave so it is a good idea for lessons to have carefully considered seating plans. Seat pupils who may need to leave a classroom quickly near to the classroom door; the further a child needs to travel from their seat to a door, the more disruption the child could cause on the way out. Disruptions, however minor, can unsettle a class for the rest of a lesson.

Children who may need a lot of direct 1:1 support (e.g. hurdle help) are best seated alone, with a vacant seat next to them. Adults, who may offer assistance, can then slip into a seat, deliver support at an appropriate height and in an appropriate manner, and then move around the classroom again, all with minimum disruption or fuss. However, make sure that this arrangement does not leave the pupil in question isolated from their peers. A child placed directly in front of a teacher's desk may become a distraction to the teacher. Allow the child to sit nearer to the sides of a room so they can be seen in peripheral vision. This allows minor behaviours to be tactically ignored.

Consideration needs to be given to pupils who have unprocessed trauma. (Unprocessed trauma is where someone has experienced a traumatic experience but has not processed it, so the feelings and responses left from the experience are still present.) Unprocessed trauma can leave pupils being hypervigilant to sound, movement and perceived threat. If the type of trauma was early interpersonal developmental (Van Der Kolk, 2005), they may perceive threat in others' actions, even if there is none. It is essential to consider the most appropriate place to seat the child to increase their sense of safety in the classroom. Positioning them towards the back of the classroom, with the other pupils in front of them, will hopefully reduce their hypervigilance. It may also be helpful to teach them the sounds of the classroom, explain that others may move around the space, and prepare them that they may see people walking past the classroom.

Other points to consider are pupils with medical needs and disabilities who may need clear access to and from and within the classroom. Another issue is meeting the needs of left-handed pupils. Think about where you put them on a table because, unlike right-handed pupils, their writing hand will cover the words as they are making them; they will therefore need wider spaces to turn their books, so that they can see the words they have written.

Adults need to be aware of the layout of their classrooms to ensure, as far as possible, the needs of all are met, so that any lesson can flow smoothly and with the minimum of disruption.

Praise the Effort

Positive reinforcement, in particular praising the effort, is an effective strategy to support positive behaviours. The basic premise of 'noticing' appropriate behaviour as opposed to inappropriate, can be considered the cornerstone to developing positive behaviour. In other words, 'say what you see'.

The regular and persistent use of praising the child's effort increases the frequency of desirable behaviours and fosters the growth of a positive self-image. When using praise, it is essential that it occurs as soon after the positive action or behaviour as possible, and that it states clearly what the child has done to be praised. Describing or noticing what the child has done will help to develop their self-worth, thus reinforcing their positive behaviours. Also, by praising the child's effort, you are embedding the positive behaviour in their brains.

Reflection Point: Time to think about my practice

Write down some 'praising the effort' statements.

When thinking about praise, try not to use the phrase 'good boy/girl', because what does 'good' mean? It is a futile term. It places the value on the child, not their behaviour. It also does not embed the wanted behaviour in their brains. The other issue is that 'good' is two-sided: if you are not 'good', you must be 'bad'; there is no in-between.

Example

Instead of saying, "Good boy, that is a beautiful picture", adults could say, "Wow, I can see you have taken great care with your drawing, and you have chosen lots of colours", or "Rachael, it looks like you are working really well with your friends and creating some incredible ideas. It shows that you are focused on your learning"

The Look

The look is a commonly used strategy, but it is often not taught to the pupils and it is assumed that the pupils will understand the meaning of the look. Making eye contact with a child will help them understand that inappropriate comments/actions they are displaying have been seen and need to be stopped. The look can communicate many different messages; however, with many strategies it needs to be taught to the pupils. The messages it can communicate to a child are:

- you are on task
- you are working hard
- keep going
- you need to settle down to your work
- you need to have a quiet voice
- you need to get on with your work
- you need to stop doing what you are doing.

We often make assumptions that pupils understand our looks and, therefore, we do not explain their meaning to them. This can lead us to become frustrated because they have not undertaken what we wanted them to do.

Therefore, we need to be clear to the pupils what we are trying to convey with the look. The pupils will need to learn what our different looks mean and need reminding of this throughout the school year. This can be done through modelling the looks at the beginning of each term, asking the pupils to practise/act them and perform the appropriate behaviours once the look has been displayed.

We need to be mindful that if we are not explicit in teaching the pupils to understand the look, then some pupils may misinterpret it and respond differently than we would hope. As parents and carers, our own children have learnt through repeatedly watching what our looks mean and this is the same for all children. However, the pupils will not have learnt each specific teacher's looks and additionally some pupils may not have experienced positive experiences around facial expressions. For some, a look may trigger an emotional or trauma response, leading to a behavioural reaction.

Therefore, they may need more explicit training about this than others. Another consideration will be pupils who have autistic spectrum disorder/condition (ASD/ASC) and other similar diagnoses. As part of their medical condition, they may not fully read and understand facial expressions. Again, provide training to understand the teacher's looks.

Privately Understood Signals

As humans, we use privately understood signals on a regular basis. There are universally understood signals, like shaking our head when we do not want someone to do something or giving a thumbs up when we are pleased with something. We indicate across the staffroom to a colleague, 'would you like a cup of tea', by either doing a 'T' signal with our fingers or cupping our hand, so it looks like it is holding a mug and bringing it up to our mouth. However, some gestures may have different meanings in other cultures so, even with universally understood signals, we need to teach them to pupils and confirm they understand what is being indicated.

A privately understood signal is generally an agreed action or word between two or more people to communicate a particular message. It can be a way of getting across a message without making it known to everyone. It is a way of reducing exposure in front of others, providing a discreet way of indicating an issue to lessen the risk of humiliation. Privately understood signals can be used in classrooms between the teaching staff to indicate that there is an issue occurring somewhere else in the classroom. This may prevent it from being highlighted to the rest of the class. It can be a word or a gesture. It does not really matter what the word or gesture is, as long the parties using the word/gesture know what it means.

Real-life example

We worked with a class staff team to establish privately understood signals to behaviourally manage the class when undertaking direct pieces of work with small groups. They would say a code word (that they had agreed together) to indicate to the other teacher that they needed to move closer to the pupils who were off task and use physical proximity to quickly address the issue. The code word on this occasion was 'spaghetti'. If the teacher said, 'there is spaghetti near the sink', the other teacher would know that there was an issue near the sink.

A privately understood signal can also be used with a child who struggles to put their hand up to ask for help, for example, if they are self-conscious and worried about being highlighted as not being able to do the work. Ideally, we would work on the child's self-confidence but, while that is developing, we need to support them. Therefore, the teacher and the child can develop a privately understood action that lets the teacher know that the child needs help. This could be the child placing a specific pen at the front of their desk or wearing a band on their wrist with a different colour on the inside, which they turn over to indicate to the teacher that they need support.

It could also be that the child needs to attend an appointment, but they do not want others to know, so the teacher and the child have a privately understood signal that indicates to the child it is time to go and provides them with a reason to leave the classroom. The teacher could give the child a 'job' to do, such as taking some papers to the front office. This discreetly allows the child to leave without the other pupils potentially asking questions.

Some pupils find it difficult to accept praise in a public or overt manner. However, it is still important to think of ways these pupils can receive praise and have their appropriate behaviour positively reinforced. This can be achieved by agreed signs and signals between the adult and child that convey positive reinforcement, but in a quiet manner. Examples could be thumbs up, light touch on the shoulder, smiles, winks and so on.

Physical proximity

Physical proximity is a useful and often discreet strategy to use. It requires the teacher to move alongside a child or a group of pupils to communicate that the behaviours that are not conducive to learning have been observed. Some pupils will correct their actions without the necessity for verbal conversation. In other cases, it may be necessary to issue a reminder of expectations (e.g. "John, you need to put your pen down and listen"). If appropriate, a light touch on a child's shoulder will indicate that the problem is with their behaviour. If touching a child is deemed inappropriate, touching chairs, desks, equipment or books belonging to a child will indicate that the issue involves them and behaviours need to be corrected or instructions followed.

The strategy is used as its name suggests. An adult 'moves in' to address a problem. If the adult needs to move across a classroom, using an individual's name is a positive approach. For instance, a teacher moves across the room saying, "John, I can see you have a problem and I am coming to help you". The issue is then dealt with. As the teacher moves away after dealing with the problem, the words may be, "Well done, John, you are now able to start your work". Moving away using a statement that reinforces the positive alternative behaviour is the 'moving out' part of the strategy. Always remember to use an appropriate position when dealing with small or seated pupils. Sit alongside pupils or crouch at the desk. Be aware of personal space issues. If it is necessary to speak to a child while both the adult and child are standing, the adult should stand to the side of the child to avoid 'blocking them in.' The adult should put their weight on a back foot and fold their hands in front of them. This is a non-threatening stance and allows for a relaxed approach to discussion/problem-solving.

Physical proximity can also be used to direct the pupils who are behaving appropriately to focus on the teacher. The teacher can stand in front of the pupils who are not on task, then they can focus their attention on the pupils who are doing as required, while praising these pupils' efforts. (These pupils should be given the teacher's attention, as they are doing what is expected.) In a sense, the teacher is using their body to 'block' the challenges, giving a clear instruction to the pupils who are off task by praising the effort of those who are on task, without directly focusing on the challenges.

As with 'the look', physical proximity may need to be taught to some pupils as they may not understand the implicit meaning or may perceive the teacher's physical proximity as a threat, leading to a behavioural response. For some pupils, physical proximity may not be a strategy to use until a positive working relationship has developed between the child and the teacher.

Tactical Ignoring

Tactical ignoring is a useful strategy for managing low-level behaviours. It can take three forms. Firstly, a particular behaviour being shown (e.g. tapping a pencil on a desk) could be ignored, but once the tapping has stopped that action could be praised. Once the child stops tapping, the response could be, "Well done, John. You have put your pencil down". We would not say, "Well done, John. You have stopped tapping your pencil", because this would remind John of what he was doing and plant it in his thoughts again. This may encourage the unwanted behaviour to start again.

Secondly, trying to tackle a number of inappropriate behaviours would, probably, lead to further difficulties with a child. On occasions, several behaviours may be displayed (e.g. rocking on a chair, making inappropriate noises and prodding another child with a pen). Choose one behaviour to address. Perhaps the behaviour chosen will not be the primary behaviour. An instruction given may be, "John, put your pen down", or "John, put the four chair legs on the floor". When the instruction is followed, praise is immediately given and another inappropriate behaviour is addressed. In the process of following a given request or instruction, then other behaviours may be corrected.

Thirdly, as discussed in physical proximity, body language can be used to 'isolate' a section of the classroom where individuals may be off task or behaving inappropriately. Praise should be given to the section of the class who are cooperating and complying and, once this is done, adults need to move around the room so as to include all sections of the classroom. Clear instructions of expectations need to follow this action and the whole class can, from that point on, be included in communication.

Tactical ignoring, as a strategy, must be carefully used. It is not always possible to ignore some behaviours shown or it may not be a suitable strategy for a particular type of child. This comes back to knowing the child in front of you. If tactical ignoring is used, make sure it is not used for too long at any one time as a child may take it as a sign of an adult accepting a particular behaviour.

Proximity Praise

This strategy emphasises a positive situation as opposed to a negative action. Often, we get pulled into focusing on the negative aspects of a situation and inadvertently give attention to the inappropriate behaviour. Unfortunately, this can reinforce the behaviour and mistakenly encourage the behaviour to happen again. In addition to positively encouraging a behaviour, we should reward the behaviour that is productive for learning. The pupils who are undertaking the behaviours that are requested/expected should receive the attention. We need to focus on the ones who are 'getting it right'.

If a child is off task or behaving inappropriately, then praising others around that child who are 'getting it right' is a positive strategy. Using this method of praise means pupils who find it difficult to manage their behaviours, begin work or stay on task are not singled out and spoken to in a negative way. By praising appropriative behaviours, other pupils who are off task observe what is expected of them and correct their own behaviours accordingly.

It can also be used if the child's driving need is to have people connected with them all the time and their learnt way of achieving this is to undertake negative behaviours. By praising pupils in close proximity, the child often engages in the wanted behaviours to have the teacher to connect with them.

Real-life example

A number of years ago, I was observing a class where the activity required the pupils to move between two areas in the classroom, depending on the correct answer to the question. I noticed that one child was going towards the wrong answer every time. Initially, I wondered if the child did not understand the task, but I quickly realised that, when the child went to the wrong area, all the other pupils and the teacher focused on them and encouraged them over to the correct area. By going to the wrong area, the child's need to have people connected to them all the time was being fulfilled.

To test my hypothesis, I asked the teacher to turn their back slightly on the child when they had gone towards the wrong answer and praise the pupils who were in the correct area. The child initially screamed at the teacher, which they tactically ignored. The child then ran to the correct area and the teacher immediately praised them. On the next question, the child went straight towards the correct answer and, again, was praised immediately.

Real-life example

When working with a Year 4 class who had been instructed to line up, there was a group of boys at the end of the line who were jiggling about. The teacher began at the front of the line, using proximity praise with all the pupils who had followed the instruction. By the time the teacher was near the group of boys, they were standing in the line as instructed and, therefore, received the praise.

This comes back to knowing the child in front of you and understanding the driving need behind the behaviours. Proximity praise, tactical ignoring and physical proximity work well together.

Processing Time

Some pupils who are given a directive or an instruction by an adult in a classroom setting cannot comply with the request immediately; they need some time to process the request and carry out the instruction given. The time allowed for the processing is known as 'take-up time'. The amount of take-up time needed will depend on the type of instruction given and the child's age. Children are constantly developing, particularly their brains, and we need to remember this when using processing time.

For a child instructed to stop tapping a pencil, the take-up time may be short. If the tapping does not stop, it may be necessary to repeat the request with a greater degree of insistence for the child to comply. Consequences may follow if instructions are not followed after the third time of asking.

If a child has not begun a task once instructions have been given, it may be necessary to allow a greater length of 'take-up time'. The 'take-up time' may actually then be termed as 'thinking time'. Thinking time allows a child to process instructions at their own pace and begin work independently of adults.

Judgements will need to be made as to how much take-up time/thinking time should be allowed to process and carry out requests. Adults should be clear with the child about the amount of time being allowed; for example, "John, you need to start work. I will give you two minutes to begin, then I will come and see how you are getting on".

When giving a child processing time, it is important to be consistent; if you have said they have two minutes, you need to give that amount of time, even if the child is continuing to do the behaviour right up to the end of the two minutes.

Real-life example

During a television programme about a school, a young person was given two minutes to hand a ball over or there would be a consequence. Throughout the two minutes, the young person bounced the ball against the wall, bounced it near the teacher and rolled it across the floor. Just before the two minutes were finished, they handed the ball over. Unfortunately, the teacher still enforced the consequence. The young person became distressed, because they had done as they were asked by handing the ball over within the two minutes. The teacher had reneged on their word.

What do you think will be the consequences for the relationship between that teacher and the young person now?

The same works the other way: if you say to the child you are coming back in two minutes, try your hardest to return within the two minutes. Classrooms are busy environments and it may not always be possible to be return in exactly two minutes, but try to make sure you acknowledge this to the child, as it will communicate that you are keeping them in mind and they are not forgotten. You could use either a privately understood signal, such as a previously agreed word or gesture to communicate this, or a look.

Hurdle Help

Hurdle help is a strategy used to help pupils get over a difficulty, usually connected with a learning issue. Some pupils faced with a clean sheet of paper can find it difficult to begin work on request. Offering a child help to begin a task can prevent them becoming disruptive or upset as a result of being unable to begin work.

Reflection Point

There could be a whole host of reasons why a child may struggle to begin a task. List some of the potential causes.

Adults can move alongside a child, preferably sitting down next to them, and give practical support; for example, "John, I will help you put the date and title on your paper". It may be necessary to give a little more support in the form of helping with ideas, spellings, reading support or perhaps writing out an example of the task set. Once the child is on task, the adult can move away. Perhaps some 'take-up time' could be given at this point to reassure a child that an adult will return to give help again, if necessary; for example, "Try questions 2 and 3, John. I will come back in two minutes and check you are managing". Again, ensure that you come back in two minutes.

Giving pupils a small task to begin their work is also helpful to a child who may struggle with several instructions or directions at one time; for instance, "John, I would like you to do question 1 and then put your hand up to let me see your work".

Real-life example

A number of years ago, we were asked to support a Year 6 child whose self-belief was very poor. He did not show his distress by externalising behaviours; he would just drop his head on the desk and refuse to do anything. His whole body oozed fear, but it could have been perceived as defiance. School and his parents were concerned for him, especially with the SATs coming up and the impending transition to secondary school. We needed to help him develop confidence in his capabilities and risk trying. Initially, we did not ask him to write, we encouraged him to play the 'squiggle game' (Winnicott, 1971). The squiggle game is a pen and paper game where one person draws a squiggle on the paper and the other person adds further drawing to the squiggle to make it into an image. This enabled him to begin putting pen to paper and, because the squiggle game cannot be perfect, it gave him permission to risk trying.

Gradually, as his confidence grew in drawing, we implemented hurdle help with his teacher. He would start every task with a quick squiggle drawing, then the teacher would write the first few words of the sentence and then the child would feel able to begin. It took lots of repetition before he was able to begin without hurdle help.

For the SATs, we taught him to start with a squiggle drawing on a separate piece of paper before he began the SATs paper. He completed all the papers, which we had been unsure he would ever attempt.

Reflection Point

Playful interactions engage pupils to risk trying.

Consider how you can introduce playful interactions in your daily practice to help pupils engage in the learning.

Broken Record

The broken record method is fundamental as a positive behaviour support technique. It is a simple but effective tool when handling difficulties in a 1:1 situation, small groups or even whole-class settings.

'You need to…' are the key words to remember when using the strategy. Using the child's name at the beginning of an instruction or direction also makes sure an individual understands they are being spoken to.

> **Example**
>
> A child walking around a classroom and not settling to a task would be instructed by the adult, "John, you need to sit down and begin your work now."
>
> If the child protests and does not comply, the adult's response may be, "John, I hear what you say, but you need to sit down now and begin the work."

The technique involves the repetition of words and instructions. Often, because the child has not followed the instruction first time or immediately, we think they have not understood us, so we change the wording of the instruction. However, if you have checked and are confident that the pupil knows what they should be doing, changing the wording of the instruction will only lead to confusion. Repeating the words provides clarity and gives the child the chance to process what you have said.

After three requests and use of the broken record strategy, it may be necessary to issue a first consequence.

> **Example**
>
> A final sentence may be, "John, you need to sit down and begin your work now or I will move you to the back of the classroom and you will need to [state the consequence appropriate to your setting]."
>
> Always praise once the broken record technique has corrected the behaviour, "Well done, John you have settled well to your work."

Real-life example

Many years ago, we were running some sessions for a group of key stage 1 pupils who had been identified as displaying their distress in challenging behaviours. One particular child was struggling to follow the instruction of sitting down on the carpet. I modelled what he needed to do by sitting cross-legged on the carpet and gave the instruction, "you need to sit on the carpet." He swore at me and screamed "No" in my face (his parents and teacher were observing through a screen). I used tactical ignoring of these behaviours and repeated, "You need to sit on the carpet." He folded his arms, then lifted his fist as if to threaten me. Again, I decided to tactically ignore these behaviours (while undertaking a dynamic risk assessment in my head) and gave the instruction again. He screamed "No" again, but sat down for about three seconds, then bounced back up.

He had done as I had asked and it did not matter that he was standing back up. I had not instructed him to sit and stay sitting on the carpet. I had just asked him to sit on the carpet, which he did, albeit for only three seconds. I then praised him for sitting on the carpet and redirected him to another activity.

This situation led to a helpful discussion with his parents and some insight in to how to manage his challenging behaviours. They said that they would have reacted to his swearing, screaming and threatening behaviours. They also noted that they would have forgotten about getting him to sit down and the whole situation would have escalated. This led to them understanding that their reactions sometimes contributed to his non-compliance with instructions and we were able to explore with them different strategies to help.

We had a number of these challenges over the sessions. Gradually, he realised we were going to be consistent, persistent and calm when an instruction was given. This enabled him to feel safe enough to let down his guard and follow the instructions. The parents mirrored this too. They later reported that it had been a turning point in their parenting, and they felt they had a stronger and more positive relationship with their little boy.

Pinball Management

This is possibly the most difficult strategy to use effectively. Adults need to be prepared, calm and well-practised in using this refocusing technique.

There may be groups of pupils in a classroom setting that can, collectively, disrupt a situation. Please hold in mind that these actions may not always be carried out consciously. When an adult speaks to one child, others may comment, interfere or antagonise a situation. This must be dealt with immediately. The adult must stay focused on the child and particular difficulty they have chosen to address.

Example

A child throws a rubber across a room and is spoken to by an adult. The child refers to an inappropriate behaviour from another child in the room so the adult then begins a conversation with a different child. This process can develop into a situation where an adult may be 'arguing' with several different pupils.

In situations where adults become distracted a refocusing technique is necessary:

- When the first child spoken to tries to draw others into the discussion, the adult's response will be, "John, I hear what you are saying, but you need to pick the rubber up now."
- If the argument with the child continues, the adult's reply is, "John, you need to pick the rubber up and settle to your work right now."
- A third attempt should be made before a formal consequence is given, "John, you need to make the right choice, pick the rubber up and start work. You will be [state the consequences appropriate in your setting] if you continue to argue and not comply."

The adult needs to stay calm, be consistent, use the appropriate body language and tone of voice and be fair in issuing any consequence. Once the request has been followed, praise must be given at the first opportunity. The outcome is often that the other pupils then refocus on the learning.

Partial Agreement

Sometimes pupils attempt to draw teaching staff into arguing and will try to have the last word. Due to feeling uncomfortable, ashamed, vulnerable or needing to be in control, a child will attempt to deny their behaviours or actions and shift the responsibility to someone else, challenging the teaching staff's judgements. Unfortunately, if teaching staff get drawn into arguing, they may fuel and continue the argument, plus escalate the behaviours. Therefore, careful modelling of not being drawn into the argument, while demonstrating that they do not have to have the last word, is essential to managing the behaviours.

Partially agreeing with the child's statement and then reminding them of the rule or expectation does not fuel the behaviour.

Example

James is swinging on his chair. The teacher gives James the clear instruction of putting all four feet of the chair on the floor, but James replies, “my brother says it can't hurt me and I can do what I like.” The teacher replies, “That may be so. In here, the rule is clear – you need to put all four feet of the chair on the floor for your safety.” Then the teacher moves away to give James time to process the instruction, modelling the expectation that the instruction will be complied with.

Reflection Point

Notice your thoughts and feelings when a child says, “My parent says I don't have to.”

Consider the following statements and write your wording to respond to each one. Then think of other statements that may arise and work out your script for those too. If you are prepared, you can respond from the thinking state instead of reacting.

”Mrs Such-&-Such says that I don't have to write today.”

”My dad says I don't have to do PE today.”

”My grandma says that I have to hit them back.”

Movement Break

During the school day, pupils are often required to sit for long periods of time and this goes against what their bodies need to do. Sometimes, pupils can get on what we call the ‘behaviour treadmill’ and seem unable to get off. Therefore, giving them a movement break can step them off the treadmill. A movement break may be asking them to get a pencil for you, for instance, or to do a job for you. Enabling pupils to physically move about may help to re-engage them in the learning.

‘Antiseptic bouncing’ is another form of movement break. It is usually used to prevent an incident or difficulty arising, rather than dealing with an incident as it occurs. If an adult can see a child becoming off task or disruptive, not cooperating and beginning to struggle to manage their behaviour in class, then antiseptic bouncing may be the tool to use to address the situation. It is low-level intervention and, used positively, it hopefully prevents a situation escalating. It additionally enables the child to have a sense of purpose and responsibility, which may change their current thinking and emotional responses.

The teacher/adults in a classroom will keep an envelope in their drawer. The envelope contains a coded message. The child is asked to go to the office or to another adult somewhere in school to deliver the envelope. (This will have been communicated with the other adult prior to using this strategy so that they know what is happening and how to respond.) Staff receiving the message realise the idea is to keep a child for a short while and then return them to the class with a 'reply'. The child is given the clear instruction of returning to their class.

When the child returns to the class the difficulties in the room that may have led to the confrontation have moved on. The teacher may then offer hurdle help to the child to support them to begin work again. Praise for taking the envelope would be appropriate and praise for settling on return will complete the use of the strategy.

Some incidents or difficulties that occur in a classroom are best dealt with in a more private setting on a 1:1 basis. Some pupils display inappropriate behaviours, and this situation can often be stimulated and reinforced by having an audience in a classroom setting. It may be more beneficial for the child to be given 'time and space' to repair, rebuild and reflect on what has occurred or be given the opportunity to do this while an event/incident is happening, rather than dealing with the issue in front of an audience.

Some pupils could have a 'Time Out' card to allow them legitimate time outside of a classroom. The 'Time Out' card is issued with a clear 'abuse it and lose it' policy. If no card is used, an adult may direct a child to leave a class. This is best done in a non-confrontational manner. For example, "John, have two minutes outside of the room to help you settle down. I will come out to see you. When you come back into the room, I will help you with your work."

When a child leaves a room, it may be necessary for an adult to accompany them to deal with a particular situation. Any issues should be dealt with as quickly as possible, with a view to a child returning to a classroom. Before returning to class, an adult may say, "Well done, John, for dealing with this issue quickly. We will both go back into class now." If an adult feels that a child may not be able to return to a lesson, plans should be in place as to how and where a child will be dealt with until the next lesson begins.

Safe Space

A 'safe space' is an area set aside in school where a child can go to regulate and have some legitimate 'time out'. The use of the space can also indicate that some 1:1 support is needed to deal with a difficult situation.

Setting up a safe space should be well planned. It is essential that the use of the space is fully understood by both the child it serves and adults in school who may be connected with the operation of the space. Ideally, it would be best in the classroom, but sometimes that may not be the appropriate space for a particular child.

The purpose and process of using a safe space must first be discussed with an individual child. If the child feels the concept of a safe space is not for them, perhaps some other strategy or means of support may need to be put in place.

Choose the safe space with the child. Walk to areas of the classroom or school and negotiate with the child where the space will be established. The child must recognise that:

(a) the area can be in their classroom or in the school

(b) the area must be inside the main school building

(c) the area must be as near to the child's classroom as possible, especially if the child is in the younger age group

(d) inside other teachers' classrooms, in halls or inside the school office are NOT areas that can be used, due to other pupils and staff needing to learn and work undisturbed

(e) if they are taught in mobile classrooms, it will not be acceptable for them to cross school playground areas; in such cases, the safe space will need to be just outside of the classroom (e.g. in the cloakroom area).

What will make up a safe space?

Once the area has been agreed, it will then be possible to begin to create the actual seating area. Two chairs, side by side, usually form the space. If there are other similar chairs set up around school, it must be clear to a pupil which areas are intended for 'safe spaces' and which areas serve other purposes (visitors to schools, areas for pupils feeling unwell, etc.). Keep the space as simple as possible.

Establishing the safe space

It must be absolutely clear to a pupil how to access and use the safe space appropriately. School staff need to agree the rules for using the space with the young person. All school staff will also need to be aware of the final arrangements for the child. If the space can be accessed during breaks and lunchtimes, lunchtime supervisor and office staff, and perhaps site supervisors, will also need to be aware of the arrangements in place. This 'whole-school knowledge' will reduce any unnecessary or inappropriate remarks being made to a child who is using their space correctly.

Taking some time to role play and practise how to use the space appropriately is an excellent strategy. This prepares the child, in advance of use and in the safety of a non-confrontational situation, to ensure they follow rules and routines for accessing the space correctly.

Using scripted language in connection with the safe space

To ensure a consistent approach to the space is established, by both the child and school staff, a form of scripted language should be developed and used.

Examples

If a child walks out of a room/lesson, the staff will direct the child by saying, "John, you need to go to your safe space. In two minutes, I will send Mrs Johnson to help you." If a teacher/member of support staff needs to direct a child to their space, to prevent issues or conflict escalating, a similar sentence would be appropriate.

Teaching a child how to appropriately ask to use their space is equally important:

Child, "Mrs Smith, I need some time out please. I want to use my safe space."

Adult, "Well done, John. You realise you need to have some time out of class. Use your safe space and I (or Mrs Johnson) will come in five minutes and help you."

Similar sentences will need to be formulated for office staff, lunchtime supervisors or any visitors to schools who may have direct contact with the focus child.

What is the action when a child has used the space appropriately?

There is one clear way to address a child who is seated at their safe space. When an adult joins them by sitting down on the spare chair, "John, well done for coming to your space and sitting and waiting for help." This acknowledges a child has made the right choice. In certain circumstances, it may be possible to give a reward, such as a simple sticker, for coming to the area as agreed. After all, this is what has been agreed and established as the strategy to use in difficult situations; a reward is therefore being given for an action successfully carried out.

Next, the adult may choose to open up a conversation with the child about why they have needed to use the safe space. "Now, John, I am guessing something is upsetting you. Tell me about it. Let us talk about what we need to do to sort this out and return to our class."

Operating the safe space

Once all arrangements, scripts and staff to support the use of the space have been identified, it will be necessary to keep the patterns of use as consistent as possible. This will, eventually, be the key to helping a pupil become more secure in school, and more able to discuss and deal with issues in a calm and controlled manner. The use of the space may become less regular once practised language and strategies become established ways of working through difficulties.

What should school staff do if they see a child using their safe space?

INITIALLY NOTHING

Leave the child to calm down and work with the nominated staff member to sort out issues and difficulties in a 1:1 situation, using scripts and techniques that the child knows and understands.

If a child is in their space without an adult, a simple 'thumbs up' could be indicated to them. The safe space should be recognised as a non-verbal communication area, except for between the pupil and nominated staff member. A staff member should always be in reserve to cover absences.

Using a safe space for pupils

Some pupils run out of lessons without knowing what 'their next choice' may be. Returning to a classroom may not be an option. They may not have the skills or the vocabulary to ask to return to class. Some pupils leave school buildings and some may choose to leave a school site. Creating a safe space is an ideal strategy to use to address such issues.

The pupil will need to know how long they have to choose a safe space to access and understand that they should not just wander the school sites aimlessly. If the space is being used for reasons of personal safety, the following points need to be considered:

(a) Set a time limit of 10 minutes for a pupil to come to the space.

(b) Ensure any staff who need to know that a pupil has left a room and is unsupervised around school, are informed as soon as possible of the situation.

(c) Send the elected member of staff to wait at the safe space for the child to come and sit down. Use the appropriate script immediately.

(d) If a child does not come as agreed after the 10-minute period, the established school procedures will need to be adopted (e.g. alert senior leadership team [SLT] members and parents; inform police if necessary).

Children should not be chased around school if they have left classrooms. Chasing can become a 'game' to a child and could be meeting the need of gaining attention or connection – even if that attention is negative. It may be necessary, at times, to follow pupils out of a classroom. Establishing and using safe spaces will reduce the need to spend time searching for the pupil and establish an appropriate strategy to use in the future.

The safe space: key points

1 The safe space must be developed and used as such and must not be used as a punishment area.

2 The space should remain exactly how it was set up for the whole time it is in use.

3 Positive scripted language should be used to communicate with a child in the safe space, whenever possible, and certainly to praise the child for using it correctly.

4 Plan, develop, establish and operate the use of the safe space carefully and consistently. Use the same staff members to support the space wherever possible.

5 Use a calm approach when working with a pupil using their space and be aware of voice levels, tones of speech and body language used in the 1:1 situation.

6 Plan and prepare for situations that may escalate if a child cannot be calmed down in the area. (Possible 'adult call card'.) Have a clear plan for summoning support.

7 Ensure all staff see the use of a safe space as a positive, supportive strategy and not as an area where a child goes to avoid work in classrooms or directions and instructions from adults.

Repair, Rebuild and Reflect

One of the most important aspects following a difficult situation is the reparation and rebuilding of the relationship between the participants. Using restorative approaches helps pupils to reflect on the situation, view it from others' perspectives and find alternative ways of responding. We all make mistakes, but the learning occurs during the reparation following the mistake. Sometimes the repair may need to occur directly after the incident but, if emotions are still running high, we sometimes need to wait.

We often expect pupils to process and repair immediately, but they may need time to emotionally settle and then begin to think things through. If the child has gone into a survival instinctive response, where adrenaline and cortisol have been released by the body, they may need up to 75 minutes to settle. Other pupils, particularly pupils who have experienced interpersonal developmental trauma and attachment disruptions, may take longer.

The other challenge often comes when we ask pupils to articulate what has happened and why they did what they did. In many cases, they may not be able to put what happened into words. Pupils with impulse control issues or who are underdeveloped in their emotional literacy, may not have the cognitive thought process to be able to verbalise what happened and the reasons for their actions, let alone discuss their feelings about it.

Reflection Point

Think of a time when you have had a heated debate with someone. Can you recall exactly what was said and done? It is unlikely that you can, because you were probably reacting in the heat of the moment. This is the case for us adults, and we have fully developed memory recall, cognitive process, verbal skills and mature emotional understanding. Therefore, when dealing with pupils, we need to consider that they are pupils less developed in these areas and may struggle to communicate what has happened.

One of the most important aspects of repairing, rebuilding and reflecting is allowing the child to express their views and allowing them to feel heard. Try to hear them first, before gently challenging their perspective if necessary. If we go straight to criticising their view, it will prevent them from being open to exploring the situation and may make them resistant to examining other situations in the future. We need to enable them to feel safe enough to risk exploring the situation, their feelings and their behavioural responses.

Another way of repairing, rebuilding and reflecting is with the use of 'think sheets'. They can be used to discuss and deal with issues in writing. The sheets support investigating incidents and mediating between pupils to ensure that there is a record of how difficulties have been resolved. Think sheets also allow every member involved in an incident to feel they have been able to put their point of view in an appropriate way and in an appropriate setting.

Think sheets can be designed to be age-appropriate; for example, using a drawing exercise for younger pupils or using toys and other objects. The sheets should be designed to cover the following areas:

1. What was the problem?
2. What were my actions?
3. What were my options?
4. What will I do in future?
5. What needs to be done now to put things right?

The completed sheets should be kept to act as evidence of how incidents were handled. All relevant information (i.e. name, date, time, others involved and mediators) should appear on the sheet.

Think sheets can be interpreted to allow staff to see if situations that affect behaviour are occurring on a regular basis. If this is the case, provision should be put in place to prevent incidents reoccurring.

However, think sheets should not be overused or the process may lose the impact desired. Think sheets are, perhaps, best used for the more serious incidents or the higher levels of inappropriate behaviours. Playground fights, swearing or intimidation towards adults may be areas where think sheets would be effective to record and, where possible, resolve issues. If used too often, pupils will also learn what they need to write to get through the task instead of using it to fully reflect on the incident and facilitate change.

There are other creative ways to repair, rebuild and reflect. Drawing, or playing it out with toys, may provide an easier way for the child to process the incident. Also, seeing a visual representation of what happened, in the drawing or with the toys, may help to facilitate change.

Storyboard technique

Draw the incident

Either the pupil or the adult (directed by the pupil) draws the sequence of the events involved in the incident on a whiteboard using comic-book style drawings. This helps to reveal the antecedent to the actual incident. (If there was more than one child involved in the incident, either see them individually or ask each child to complete their view of the sequence of the events.)

Draw an alternative ending

Ask the pupil to rub out the first drawing and get them to draw what could have been done differently; always discuss what the outcome would likely be. You can ask them to think of other solutions, including how to manage their feeling responses.

Playing-it-out technique

This uses small figures or characters, which could be animals, peoples, cars or similar. Ask the pupil to choose figures to represent those involved in the incident. Then ask them to show you what happened by moving the figures. Next, ask how the figures are feeling at the end of the event. Sometimes it is better to ask how the toys are feeling and not to directly ask the child how they are feeling. Children (even teenagers) find the symbolic distance of discussing the toy's feelings easier than owning the feeling themselves.

Finally, ask the child to play out what could be done differently. Let them play it out, even if it is not a successful solution, then ask them again how the toys are feeling. Keep encouraging them to consider other solutions, until they come to a satisfactory resolution for all. Some pupils may need suggestions to find a different approach. It is important to gently offer these different approaches, rather than insisting on them; our experience is that if a child comes to a solution themselves, they are more likely to implement it.

As per the storyboard technique, if there is more than one child involved in the incident, allow each child to have their turn showing what happened. Then they could look at different options individually or, if they are settled enough, they could jointly find a solution.

Changing Mindsets

Changing mindsets is an important strategy for supporting behaviour for all parties when dealing with challenging behaviours. Sometimes, individuals' mindsets get stuck in a viewpoint and this frame of mind then influences their behaviours. Therefore, having understanding to the cause or need driving the behaviour and using strategies can change their mindset, thus leading to behavioural changes. Humour is part of the art of teaching. Classrooms need to be places to educate, but also have elements of fun. Using humour can help de-escalate difficult situations that may develop anywhere in school throughout the day. Adults must ensure that remarks made in a humorous way are taken in a similar vein and do not appear as sarcastic remarks to others.

Humour is, perhaps, the most intuitive intervention. Knowing and understanding a child before humour is used to de-escalate a situation is crucial. When used in the right way, at the right time and in the right spirit, humour is a valuable and useful tool to manage difficult situations.

Distraction is also a helpful technique for changing mindsets. Sometimes, just talking about a subject that we know the child likes can help regulate them and change their thinking. On other occasions, it could be that we use tactical ignoring and begin having a conversation with a colleague. The conversation could be about more or less anything appropriate, for example, a TV programme that we know the child might be interested in. It gives the child time to settle, while also allowing them to change their focus to what the adults are talking about. Before long, they may try to engage in the conversation. If they are responding to the conversation, it means they are beginning to come back into their thinking brain and are de-escalating.

Verbal communication: "I" and "You" messages

We can influence mindset by the way we communicate with a child. Being aware of the communication process, both verbal and non-verbal, will support changing the mindset. Being aware of body language, tone of voice and our style of approach will all have an effect on how successful a strategy might be. An example of changing the mindset with verbal communication is the use of the "I" message. This is an attempt to focus on the behaviour rather than the child as the issue of concern. It contrasts with "You" messages, which are blaming and judgemental:

> *"You are ... disobedient/thoughtless/selfish/lazy/inconsiderate."*

These judgements do not distinguish between the child and the behaviour. The "I" message, on the other hand, describes how "I" am feeling and then describes the behaviour that has led to these feelings:

"I feel ... disappointed/let down/put upon/annoyed when you forget to do your homework."

The messages can be depersonalised even further by substituting 'pupils' for 'you':

"I feel let down when pupils don't keep the rules about running in the corridor that we have all agreed."

"I" messages can also be used when we are praising pupils. Dweck's work (1999) suggests that praise that is directed to the behaviour, rather than to the inherent qualities of the child, leads to more persistence in the face of difficulty or challenge.

"I" messages do not come easily – they need to be consciously practised, particularly in the face of inappropriate behaviour. The "I" message is made up of three parts:

- "When you ..." Behaviour
- "I feel ..." Feeling
- "Because ..." Reason for the feeling

An effective "I" message acknowledges a problem and opens the way to search for a solution. It communicates feelings, reduces the likelihood of confrontation, opens up the possibility of discussion, protects the self-concept of the child, and allows the adult to stay in control and express feelings.

Sensory-based interventions

Another way of changing mindsets is by using sensory materials to help the child to regulate. Sensory materials can be anything that stimulates the senses. If a child is responding from a survival instinctive response, the part of the brain that is fully alert is the lower brain stem. This part of the brain responds to sensory input. Using sensory materials can allow the pupil to settle, regulate and return to a calm state. Let us just consider this from an adult point of view: when we are upset or dysregulated, we often go for a walk, make a drink or fiddle with some sensory materials such as fabric or worry beads. These are all sensory ways of regulating.

Some people seem to believe that, by allowing the pupil to do playful/sensory tasks, the challenging behaviours are being rewarded. However, the aim of any intervention or strategy is to help the pupil to return to a regulated state and be ready for learning again. If using some sensory materials helps the pupil to settle, and they can then return to the classroom, the strategy has done its job. Other strategies which do not involve sensory play can be used during calm times to prevent behaviours happening again. Occupational therapy advice may be useful to seek to support individual pupil's needs.

Real-life example

While undertaking an observation of a pupil, it became apparent that she was becoming more and more distressed as the session went by. The more distressed she felt, the more challenging her behaviour became. She began throwing books around the classroom, leaving the classroom and shouting back through the door. In the corridor she began pulling things out of storage cupboards and throwing them. The teachers were using tactical ignoring, but this strategy was not appropriate for this pupil as the driving need behind the behaviours was to stay connected to others. So, she escalated the behaviours until adults had to respond for safety reasons and, finally, she got what she needed.

It was suggested to the teacher that, before it got to the point where somebody was hurt by the pupil's behaviours, some sensory materials were provided for her. The teacher remembered that the pupil liked playing with slime. They gave her some slime to play with and, within a few minutes, they could see her visibly relaxing. Within the play, the staff were also able to help her use all her senses, including the vestibular and proprioceptive senses. The vestibular sense is the body's ability to interpret the sensory information controlling eye movements and balance. It is important in helping to understand where our body is in space and helps with regulating ourselves. The proprioceptive sense informs the body of its position. It plays a significant role in regulating ourselves, body awareness and co-ordination. They asked her to smell it, rub it on the back of her hand, push it hard onto the table and scrape it back off. They encouraged her to balance on one leg while playing with it, to walk on tiptoes while balancing the slime on her hands and to cross it from one hand to another. This sensory activity became part of the pupil's individual behaviour plan and her daily routine: it helped her to self-regulate and, therefore, she was better able to behave appropriately in the learning environment and access the teaching.

Reflection Point

It may sound easy to spot that the driving need is to stay connected to others, but it is often not so straightforward in practice because, when the teachers try to meet the pupil's need, the pupil rejects their attempts. This can leave teachers feeling confused and unsure about what strategy to use. Sometimes, the driving need behind behaviours is difficult to identify.

Top Tips for Using Positive Behaviour Support Techniques

1 Know the pupils in front of you. Build a relationship with them.

2 Stay calm and remain in control of situations. Know yourself and understand your own triggers.

3 Use a graded and gradual approach to selecting a strategy to use.

4 Praise at the first opportunity once the wanted behaviour happens: 'Catch them being good.'

5 Be aware of body language, words used, styles of approach, tone of voice and voice levels when handling any difficulty.

6 Give positive reminders and expectations of how to get things right at every opportunity.

7 Avoid situations developing into confrontational issues. (If you fight fire with fire, you may get more fire.)

8 Work towards a 'win–win' situation when managing difficult situations.

9 Separate a pupil from a behaviour: it is the behaviour that is unacceptable, not a pupil. Hold the pupil, their developmental stage and the context in mind – this helps you to stay in your regulated stage.

10 Allow pupils to calm down before having a 1:1 conversation after difficult incidents.

11 Have a 'new lesson – new start' or 'new day – new start' policy when dealing with incidents.

FINAL THOUGHTS

At the beginning of this book, we stated that our main aim was to provide the reader with a process, not just for managing behaviour, but for understanding it as well. In writing this book, we have solidified our thinking, knowledge, skills and professional practice to provide a holistic approach to understanding and supporting behaviour. We hope this has been the experience for the reader as well.

The approaches described have been inspired by the pupils we have had the honour to teach and support over many years. They have been our greatest teachers. Each one of them has come with their own experiences and view of the world, and every single one of them has helped us to develop as people and as educators. Some have challenged our thinking, our resilience and made us question our skills, but they have each helped us to reflect and evolve. From the little person who taught us to be patient and wait for him to come to us as he was too scared to connect to another human, to the little person who left us holding her head up high and with a full head of hair, after arriving into our school with bald patches on her scalp where she had been pulling chunks of hair out to show her distress and fear about learning. Furthermore, we have been influenced by the most wonderful and dedicated professional practitioners who, every day, make a significant and lasting difference to the pupils they support and teach. We count ourselves so fortunate to have both been in occupations that we love, but to have also had such incredible teachers (pupils and adults) that have educated and influenced us.

While placing an importance on the reasons for and issues behind the behaviour enables us to be fully confident in our responses to it, we have also attempted to explore the practical strategies and interventions that are needed to develop appropriate responses. But more than that, we have provided a process that allows the practitioner to ask themselves questions about their own viewpoint with regard to behaviour, their existing behaviour support approaches and the effectiveness of them. We all have strategies in our toolbag, but there is always room for more. We feel that the bigger the toolbag the more likely we can support the variety and diversity of need.

But, to allow for greater effectiveness and increase the chances of success, it is important to ask some fundamental questions before implementation:

- What is the underlying need?
- Why did we choose that strategy and/or intervention?

- How do we implement it?
- When do we implement it?
- How do we know it will be effective?

Each section of the book has been an attempt to provide some of the answers to these questions. The questions may seem simple, but the answers are complicated; therefore, topics or themes as varied as influences on behaviour, target-setting, culture and ethos, definition, relationships and types of behaviour all deserve exploration.

Each chapter looks at ways of gathering as much information as possible about the behaviour, so that affecting change and providing support comes from an informed position instead of a reactive stance.

However, all chapters should be read with the aim of developing responses to behaviour appropriate to the specific need of the individual pupil.

It is important to note that these responses, strategies and interventions, and the examination of the process to implement them, are not about a particular cohort of pupils: they are for all pupils. Pupils are individuals, each with their own specific needs. The influences on their behaviour will be particular to them, the reasons behind the behaviour will be specific to them, and the function of and drives for the behaviour will be individual to them. All behaviours on the spectrum we describe, be they of low, medium or high intensity, deserve support and a planned, measured response.

All elements of developing responses to behaviour, from policy through to practice, should be about all pupils in the school. Culture and ethos, boundaries, target-setting and expectations should take into account the needs of all in the learning environment, not be based on a few individuals or a cohort. We would like to be clear that, when we use the phrase 'understanding behaviour', we are not condoning, tolerating or excusing inappropriate or harmful actions. But we are asking the practitioner to go beyond and behind the behaviour, to give themselves the information needed to respond and not react. Educators who reflect and respond, rather than react, are more likely to facilitate a learning environment that promotes growth and development. We believe the suggestions in this book help with that process.

The government issued a range of new guidance that was implemented in September 2022. This included new directives for headteachers and staff on behaviour (DfE, 2022). The introduction states, 'good behaviour is central to a good education', 'positive behaviours are more likely by proactively supporting pupils … some pupils will need additional support to reach the expected standard', and 'schools should be able to respond promptly, predictably and with confidence … and consider how such behaviour can be prevented' (DfE, 2022).

We totally agree with these sentiments, that behaviour support approaches need to be proactive rather than reactive. The new DfE guidance supports this by stating 'adjustments should be made proactively and by design' (DfE, 2022). There may be times when we miss the trigger and need to dynamically assess the situation, but best practice would be to start with a planned response developed from the process outlined in this book. The strategies and interventions, and the idea of viewing behaviour on a spectrum, are offered within the context of using them at a preventative level first, and then implementing responses based on the needs of the pupil, the context in which the behaviour is occurring, trying to understand the behaviour, and then offering and implementing support. All this is underpinned by a culture and ethos that promote a learning environment where good behaviour can flourish, behaviours of concern are identified early and change supported.

In conclusion, this book offers a template by which behaviour support approaches can be implemented on a 1:1 basis or with a group. It is intended for the practitioner to build on the suggestions and practical solutions offered. We recognise that the professionals working directly with pupils are the experts on the particular pupils in their schools. We hope they can take the template we have provided and build on it when developing their responses to the behaviours they are experiencing and the pupils who need their support.

References

Acharya, S. & Shukla, S., 2012, 'Mirror Neurons: Enigma of the Metaphysical Modular Brain', *Journal of Natural Science, Biology and Medicine*, 3 (2), pp.118–124.

Bambaeeroo, F., & Shokrpour, N., 2017, 'The Impact of the Teachers' Non-Verbal Communication on Success in Teaching'. *Journal of Advances in Medical Education & Professionalis*m, 5, pp. 51-59.

Bandura, A., 1977, *Social Learning Theory*, General Learning Press, New York.

Bell, K., ed. 2013. "behavior." In *Open Education Sociology Dictionary*. Retrieved December 31, 2022 (https://sociologydictionary.org/behavior/).

Bennett, T., 2017, 'Creating a Culture: How School Leaders Can Optimise Behaviour', *Independent Review of Behaviour in Schools* [online], Crown, London, https://www.gov.uk/government/uploads/system/uploads/attachment_data/file/602487/Tom_Bennett_Independent_Review_of_Behaviour_in_Schools.pdf [accessed 17 April 2022].

Buechner, C. W. *1971 quoted in Evans, R.L.,1971, Richard Evans' Quote Book ("Selected from the 'Spoken Word' and 'Thought for the Day' and from many inspiring thought-provoking sources from many centuries") Quote Page 244, Column 2, Publishers Press, Salt Lake City, Utah. (Verified with scans; thanks to the librarians of Harold B. Lee Library, Brigham Young University, Provo, Utah)*

Cambridge University Press, 2022a, 'Presence', *Cambridge Dictionary* [online], https://dictionary.cambridge.org/dictionary/english/presence [accessed 26 August 2019].

Cambridge University Press, 2022b, 'Culture', *Cambridge Dictionary* [online], https://dictionary.cambridge.org/dictionary/english/culture [accessed 17 August 2022].

Cambridge University Press, 2022c, 'Policy', *Cambridge Dictionary* [online], https://dictionary.cambridge.org/dictionary/english/policy [accessed 17 April 2022].

Cambridge University Press, 2022d, 'Intervention', *Cambridge Dictionary* [online], https://dictionary.cambridge.org/dictionary/english/intervention [accessed 28 December 2022].

Cannon, W. B., 1915, *Bodily changes in pain, hunger, fear, and rage*. New York: Appleton-Century-Crofts. p. 211.

Canter, L. & Canter, M., 1992, *Assertive Discipline: A Take-Charge Approach For Today's Educator*, 2nd edition Canter and Associates, Santa Monica.

Center on the Developing Child at Harvard University, 2017, Serve and Return http://developingchild.harvard.edu/science/key-concepts/serve-and-return/ [accessed 1 July 2017].

Cerio, J., 2000, *Play Therapy: A Do-It-Yourself Guide for Practitioners.* Lea R. Powell Institute for Children and Families, New York.

Children Act, 1989, Available at https://www.legislation.gov.uk/ukpga/1989/41/contents accessed on 27 August 2022.

Committee of Enquiry, 1989, *The Elton Report: Discipline in Schools* [online], Her Majesty's Stationary Office, London, http://www.educationengland.org.uk/documents/elton/ [accessed 17th April 2022].

Cotton, D., 2017, *How to Teach Behaviour and How Not to*, Create Space Independent Publishing Platform, Scotts Valley.

Cozolino, L., 2013, *The Social Neuroscience of Education*, W.W. Norton & Company, New York.

Cuddy, A., 2012, 'Your Body Language May Shape Who You Are' [TED Talk], TedGlobal, Available at https://www.ted.com/talks/amy_cuddy_your_body_language_may_shape_who_you_are?language=en, accessed on 22 August 2022..

Cuddy, A.J.C., Wilmuth, C.A. & Carney, D.R., 2012, 'The Benefit of Power Posing Before a High-Stakes Social Evaluation', Harvard Business School Working Paper, No. 13-027, https://dash.harvard.edu/bitstream/handle/1/9547823/13-027.pdf Accessed on 28 December 2022.

Delahook, M., 2019, *Beyond Behaviours: Using Brain Science and Compassion to Understand and Solve Children's Behavioural Challenges*, PESI Publishing and Media, Eau Claire.

Delaney. M., 2009, *Teaching the Unteachable: Practical Ideas to Give Teachers Hope and Help when Behaviour Management Strategies Fail: What Teachers Can Do when All Else Fails*, Worth Publishing.

Department for Education (DfE), 2011, *Teacher's Standards: Guidance for School Leaders, School Staff and Governing Bodies*, Secretary of State for Education, London, https://assets.publishing.service.gov.uk/government/uploads/system/uploads/attachment_data/file/1040274/Teachers__Standards_Dec_2021.pdf

Department for Education and Department of Health, (2015) *Special educational needs and disability code of practice: 0 to 25 years*. Available at: https://www.gov.uk/government/publications/send-code-of-practice-0-to-25 (Accessed: 27 December 2022).

Department for Education (DfE), 2022, *Behaviour in Schools, available at* https://www.gov.uk/government/publications/behaviour-in-schools--2 accessed on 29 August 2022

Dickerson, J. T., 2019, *Cause I ain't got a pencil*, Jax Productions, Decatur.

Dix, P., 2017, *When the Adults Change Everything Changes: Seismic Shifts in School Behaviour*, Independent Thinking Press, Carmarthen.

Dwivedi, K.N. (ed.), 1997, *The Therapeutic Use of Stories*, Routledge, London.

Forbes, H.T. & Post, B.B., 2006, *Beyond Consequences, Logic and Control: A Love Based Approach to Helping Children with Severe Behaviours*, Volume 1, Beyond Consequences Institute, Orlando.

French, L. & Klein, R. (eds), 2012, *Therapeutic Practice in Schools: Working with the Child within: A Clinical Workbook for Counsellors, Psychotherapists and Arts Therapists*, Routledge, London.

Ginnot, H., 1972, *Teacher and Child: A Book for Parents and Teachers*, Macmillan Company, New York.

Jung, C.G., 1954, *The Development of Personality*, Routledge, London.

Landreth, G., 2012, *Play Therapy: The Art of the Relationship. (3rd Edition)* Routledge, New York.

Maslow, A. H., 1954, *Motivation and personality*, Harper and Row, New York.

Maslow, A, H., 1966, *The Psychology of Science: A Reconnaissance*. Harper & Row, New York.

Mehrabian, A., 1981, *Silent messages: Implicit communication of emotions and attitudes* (2d ed.). Belmont, Wadsworth Pub.

Morgan, N., 2013, *Blame My Brain: The Amazing Teenage Brain Revealed*, Walker Books, London.

Murray, S., 2014, 'A play development programme for schools'. Northampton. Unpublished document.

Murray, S., 2017, 'A Written Evaluation of the Nature and Impact of Relational Trauma and Loss upon a Pupil and the Development of an Attachment Aware and Trauma Informed School Environment', University of Brighton. Unpublished paper

Murray, S., 2020, Therapeutic Games to Treat Anxieties and Fears. In J. Stone & C. E. Schaefer, eds. *Game Play Therapy for Treating Specific Problem Behaviors of Youth (3rd edition),* Hoboken, John Wiley & Sons, pp.155 -171

Oaklander, V., 1988 [1978], *Windows to Our Children: A Gestalt Therapy Approach to Children and Adolescents*, Gestalt Journal Press.

Olson, K., 2014, *The Invisible Classroom: Relationships, Neuroscience and Mindfulness in Schools*, W.W. Norton and Company, New York.

Oxford Learner's Dictionary. 2022 Behaviour, Oxford Learner's Dictionary (online) https://www.oxfordlearnersdictionaries.com/definition/english/behaviour [accessed on 28 December 2022]

Porges, S., 2011, *The Polyvagal Theory*, W.W. Norton, New York.

Rodenburg, P., 2009, *Presence: How to Use Positive Energy for Success in Every Situation*, Penguin, London.

Rogers, B., 2011, *Classroom Behaviour: A Practical Guide to Effective Teaching, Behaviour Management and Colleague Support*, Volume 3, Sage Publications Ltd, London.

Salter, R., 2016, *Classroom Presence Pocketbook*, Teachers' Pocketbooks, Alresford.

Siegel, D.J., 2010, *Mindsight*, Bantam, Oxford.

Team Teach., 2019, *Team Teach Workbook*, Team Teach, London.

Temple, S., 2005, 'Teachers are Young People's Leaders', *Emotional Literacy Update*, September (20), pp.10-11.

Van Der Kolk, B. A., 2005, Developmental trauma disorder: Toward a rational diagnosis for children with complex trauma histories. *Psychiatric Annals*, 35, 401–408.

Walker, P., 2013, *Complex PTSD: From Surviving to Thriving*. Lafayette, CA: Azure Coyote Publishing

Wilson, A., Passik, S. D., & Faude, J. P. (1990) Self-regulation and its failures. In J.Masling (Ed.), Empirical Studies in Psychoanalytic Therapy, Vol. 3 (pp. 149-213) Hillsdale, NJ: The Analytic Press. Cited in Schore, A. (2012) Affect Regulation and the Origin of the Self: The Neurobiology of Emotional Development. London: Routledge

Winnicott, D.W., 1971, *Therapeutic Consultations: Child Psychiatry*, Basic Books, Inc., New York.

Hinton House Publishers
Books and resources for education, special needs, therapy and social care
Available on amazon
THE BEREAVEMENT BOOK
ACTIVITIES TO SUPPORT CHILDREN AND YOUNG PEOPLE THROUGH GRIEF AND LOSS
TINA RAE
PROMOTING POSITIVE BODY IMAGE IN TEENAGERS
ESSENTIAL EVIDENCE-BASED STRATEGIES AND RESOURCES
TINA RAE & ALI D'AMARIO
A TOOLBOX of WELLBEING
Supporting Children through Grief & Loss
Practical Ideas and Creative Activities for Schools & Carers
Anna Jacobs
SUPPORTING ADOLESCENTS & TEENAGERS WITH STRESS & ANXIETY
A practical guide
Tina Rae
Mindfulness Activity Cards for Children and Teens
Understanding & Supporting Children & Young People with Emotionally Based School Avoidance (EBSA)
TINA RAE
101 Activities for Social & Emotional Resilience
Sue Jennings
hintonpublishers.com
HINTONHOUSE